Beginning Racquetball:
A Primer

SECOND EDITION

Cheryl Norton, Ed.D.

Associate Professor of Human Performance
Metropolitan State College of Denver

James E. Bryant, Ed.D.

Professor of Human Performance
San Jose State University

Morton Publishing Company
925 W. Kenyon Ave., Unit 12
Englewood, Colorado 80110

Printed in the United States of America

ISBN: 8-89582-218-0

Preface

Beginning Racquetball: A Primer is designed for the novice and beginning player attempting to develop skills in racquetball. The text is divided into ten chapters that deal with the basics of racquetball.

The first two chapters present information on equipment, safety, preliminaries to the strokes in racquetball and an introduction to the game of racquetball. Chapters three and four introduce the various offensive and defensive strokes used in playing racquetball. These are the basic strokes that enable the player to engage in a competitive experience. Chapter five provides information on putting the ball into play by serving the ball, and chapter six introduces how to cope with the back wall and the corners of the racquetball court when the ball is in play. Chapters seven and eight serve as a culmination of the first six chapters by providing insight on how to put all the strokes together in a plan of offensive and defensive strategy.

Chapters nine and ten complete the overall view of a primer for racquetball. Chapter nine gives insight on drills that provides the student with drills for practice. Chapter ten establishes the basis to the game by introducing the rules and etiquette of racquetball.

The text is an appropriate introduction to racquetball for the novice player and it will serve as a guide to enable the novice to develop both physical and mental skills needed to succeed in racquetball. Through the use of photographs and illustrations the concept of the game is visually presented to aid in comprehending the skills of the game. The summary sections entitled "points to remember" and "common errors and how to correct them" enhance the learning experience for the player. Overall, the text provides a solid primer of information and insight for the novice or beginning player.

Acknowledgments

The contributions of many individuals provided the input needed to complete this book.

Catherine A. Busalacchi, Recreation Coordinator for the San Jose State University Events Center and a championship level competitive racquetball player, is acknowledged for her suggestions and cooperation during the development of this edition. Jane Kober, Assistant Professor of Human Performance, Metropolitan State College of Denver, is also recognized for her thoughtful insight and creative efforts associated with the chapter on drills. A very special thanks and acknowledgment to Ron and Joni McCall, Lydia Hammock, Mark Diaz, and David Garcia for their modeling of the various strokes and situations. The illustrations, prepared by Darryl Wisnia, added greatly to the understanding of the material concerning strategies, court dimensions and drills.

Schoeber's Athletic Club, San Jose, California, is recognized for permitting photographs to be taken of skill and play situations in its club racquetball facilities.

Table of Contents

Chapter One   — Court, Equipment, and Safety   1

Chapter Two   — Introduction and Preliminaries
                 to the Strokes in Racquetball   9

Chapter Three — Offensive Strokes   27

Chapter Four   — Defensive Strokes   41

Chapter Five   — Serves in Racquetball   51

Chapter Six   — Use of Back Wall and Corners   65

Chapter Seven — Putting the Strokes Together:
                 Non-Thinking Strategy   75

Chapter Eight — Putting the Strokes Together:
                 Thinking Strategy   83

Chapter Nine   — Drills for the Player   91

Chapter Ten   — Court Etiquette and
                 Interpreting the Rules 103

Glossary of Terms in Racquetball 115

Official American Amateur
Racquetball Association Rules 119

Index 135

CHAPTER 1

Court, Equipment, and Safety

Racquetball is played in an enclosed court using the four walls, floor, and ceiling as the playing surface. In areas where a four-wall court cannot be built, one- or three-wall racquetball may be played. The rules and strategy for all these games are similar. This text, however, will concentrate only on the more complex, four-wall game.

The dimensions and markings on the court are as shown on the following page. Fortunately, the terminology used to describe the court is easily learned: floor, ceiling, front, back, and side walls. The floor lines identify the **service zone** (bounded by the service line and short line), two rectangular areas called **service boxes** and the drive serve lines. The only other mark on the court denotes the **receiving line** for the player returning the serve.

BRIEF OVERVIEW OF THE GAME

The object of the game of racquetball is to score 15 points before your opponent does. Only the serving player scores points. A point is scored when the server's opponent fails to hit the ball to the front wall before the ball touches the floor twice. If the server fails to return the ball to the front wall, the server loses serve. In this way, service (and the opportunity to score) is alternated until one player or team accumulates 15 points and wins the game.

Racquetball may be played with two (singles), three (cut-throat), or four (doubles) players. In singles, one player opposes another player, and in doubles, one two-person team plays another two-person team. However, in cut-throat, a single server plays against two opponents. When the server loses serve, one of the opponents becomes the server and plays against the remaining two players. The first player to earn 15 points is the winner.

In all games, each rally (exchange of hits between opposing players) is begun with a **legal serve**. For the serve to be legal, the server must stand in the service zone, drop the ball to the floor, and strike it on the rebound so that it hits the front

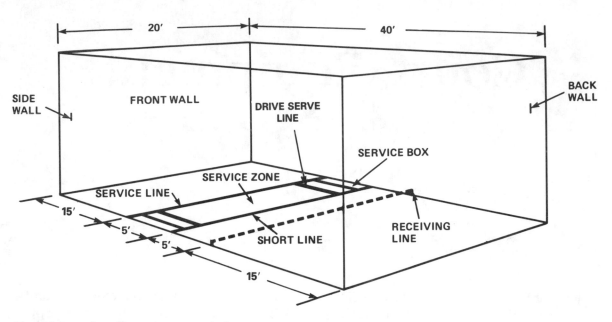

Dimensions and markings on a racquetball court.

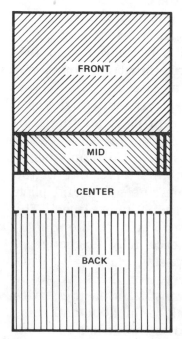

Designated floor areas on the court.

wall before any other court surface. The front wall rebound may not touch the floor in front of or on the short line. Before the ball hits the floor, it may rebound off one side wall but not off the ceiling, back wall, or both side walls. However, the return of serve and any other hit may rebound the ball off any surface except the floor before reaching the front wall. Service is changed when the server fails to keep the ball in play or he/she does not serve legally. If the receiver fails to return the ball to the front wall, a point is scored.

OUTFITTING FOR PLAY

Dress

The usual dress for both men and women includes a sports shirt or T-shirt and shorts.

Head or wristbands aid in the absorption of perspiration around the head and hands and are optional to wear. Shirts will help to absorb body perspiration and must be worn at all times during play. Body perspiration dripping onto the floor of the court provides a potential hazard to cutting and turning associated with footwork.

Racquetball court shoe suitable for racquetball.

Racquetball head and wrist bands.

Shoes

The footwear worn on a racquetball court should be an athletic shoe that supports shifting body weight and lateral movement on the court. Racquetball court shoes are made specifically for players who take the game seriously. Tennis shoes and basketball shoes can also be worn by a player, but they are a secondary alternative to the court shoe. Shoes designed for running should never be used, and dark soled shoes are also restricted since they mar court surfaces. A court shoe should have excellent traction. Gum rubber soles provide that traction. Shoes should also

have a full length midsole for proper cushioning, ventilation and lateral support. A reminder for proper footwear includes wearing athletic socks with your court shoe to prevent the foot from sliding in the shoe and creating blisters.

Gloves

The use of a glove is optional and dependent upon your comfort and need. Many players wear a glove on their

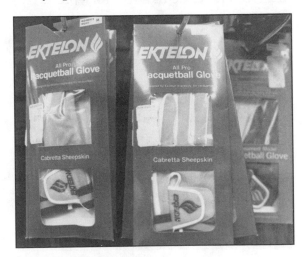

Racquetball gloves.

racquet hand to help maintain a better grip on the racquet and prevent the racquet from slipping from their hand.

Protective Eyewear

Lensed eyewear designed for racquet sports is required by the rules of racquetball and the reputable management of any court facility. Lensed eyewear is now developed for the player who wears corrective lenses and the player who does not wear glasses. Severe eye damage, including detached retinas and the loss of vision, have followed direct eye hits with either the ball or racquet. Proper protective eyewear dramatically reduces the possibility of eye injury.

Basic features of protective eyewear includes the selection of a lens that is distortion free and provides peripheral vision. Lens should be treated to eliminate fogging, and the frame should have shock resistant nose and forehead padding. A polycarbonate lens resists shattering and is the recommended lens for protective eyewear.

Protective eyewear.

Ball

Specifications for a racquetball ball are determined by the American Amateur Racquetball Association. Balls come in several colors, but most are blue.

Racquetball balls.

Racquets

The selection of a racquet is dependent upon the style of play, skill level and the amount of money you want to invest. The frame of the racquet is constructed of either a metal alloy (typically aluminum) or a composite of high-technology fibers such as graphite, boron and fiberglass. The aluminum racquet tends to be less expensive and generally quite durable. They are produced with a full range of flexibility and maintain a good feel and playability. Composite racquets tend to have the highest power indexes. The composite of graphite, boron and fiberglass contributes

Selection of racquets.

to power, reinforcement of stress areas, and dampening of racquet vibrations.

Modern technology has gone beyond racquets made of composite materials as the singular feature. Racquets are now produced in midsize (75-85" string area and 19-19¾" length) and oversize (85-95" string area and 20-21" length). Head shapes continually change. They presently tend to be a tear shape configuration. The throat area of a racquet is usually defined as closed or wishbone. The sweet spot of racquets is much larger with the change to mid size and oversized shapes. These sweet spots are elongated and cover a larger width than the original "normal" size racquet.

Grip Size

As a rule of thumb, the grip size should be smaller than that of a tennis racquet.

Grip sizes range from super small to a medium size. Most experts suggest that when gripping the racquet properly, the middle finger of the racquet hand should just touch the palm at the base of the thumb, to allow for a good wrist snap and racquet control.

Racquet Strings and Tension

Racquets are often already strung when you buy them. When a racquet is strung or restrung you need to specify the amount of tension. Tension levels are recommended with information accompanying a new racquet, but if you select a tension level it should range from 30 to 50 pounds. On the average, most players opt for a tension level of 40-45 pounds.

Handle and Thong:

Racquet handle grips are made of rubber or leather. Although leather is more expensive if tack treated, it usually allows you to grip the racquet more securely. When selecting a racquet, look for a handle that dampens vibration and reduces wrist fatigue.

To be legal, each racquet must have a **thong** attached to the handle. The thong is a safety cord that is worn on the wrist during play. Replacement thongs may be purchased where racquetball equipment is supplied.

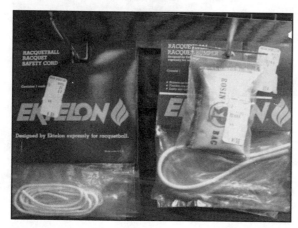

Replacement safety thongs.

Care

Racquets are easy to care for if you use some common sense. Try not to leave your racquet in the backseat of your car. Extremes in heat or cold will cause the strings to become brittle or break down faster. Keep a cover on the racquet to prevent objects from catching in the strings. If your strings are breaking frequently,

plastic eyelets inserted where the string wraps around the frame to protect the strings from wearing on the edge may prevent breaking.

SAFETY ON THE COURT

Safety on the court begins when you walk onto the court, put on your lens eyewear, and shut the door to protect against people walking in during play. During play, a racquetball court is safe only if all the players are courteous. This means staying out of your opponent's path to the ball or arm swing. Similarly, no shot is "too good to pass up" if a player is in the path of your swing. There is no excuse for hitting another player with your racquet. If a player is that close to you, your shot could not have been clear. In addition, learn to play the strokes correctly. Too many players keep their tennis stroke alive

Hitting a ball when your opponent is in the way.

in the racquetball court. Wide swings from the shoulder require the room that a tennis court provides. There is no place on the racquetball court for this kind of play.

As mentioned earlier, each racquet must have a thong or safety cord attached to it. This cord is worn around the wrist of the playing hand to prevent the racquet from flying out of the hand of the player and injuring someone on the court. This cord must be used at all times.

Finally, you should continually be aware of players' movements on the court. Stay out of the way of the player hitting the ball, and when it is your turn to hit, take your shot only if it is clear. Most balls are hit from the back of the court forward. If you are in front of the ball, DO NOT turn completely around to "see" what is going on behind you in the back court. This not only exposes your chest and abdomen to a hard-hit ball, but it leaves your face unprotected. Rather, you should angle your body slightly so that you can see the back court with your peripheral vision and hold the racquet to protect your face as you look through the strings. Using the racquet to protect your face from an oncoming ball is an effective safety measure only if the racquet "beats" the ball to the target. Don't rely on your reflexes to "get the racquet" up in time to protect your face. As a precaution, you can use your racquet as a shield if your face is exposed to the ball's path, and you must always wear your protective eyewear to protect your eyes against the stray shot. This way you can play the game and finish "looking" the same way as when you entered the court.

You should be aware that experienced players will let the ball rebound off the

Protecting your face by looking through the racquet strings.

back wall before playing it. This means that a center court position needs to be held open for that player to follow the ball. Anticipate the most direct path to the ball that your opponent can take, and keep that court position clear. Racquetball is not a game that allows mental lapses. Each player must know where the ball is at all times and where the other players are moving.

Should you interfere with your opponent's movement on the court, completion of that player's swing, or get hit with your opponent's racquet, a **hinder** must be called. A hinder should be called by the offended player in a recreational game and by a referee during tournament play. When a hinder is called, play is stopped and the point re-played from the serve. Contact does not have to occur for a hinder to be requested. Preferably, play

Player not leaving center court to give opponent clear shot off a back wall rebound.

should stop before players or racquets collide in order to avoid potential injury.

Safety is a matter of habit and thinking: protect yourself by wearing lensed eyewear, using your racquet as a shield, keeping your thong on your wrist, and closing the door of the court when playing. Anticipate your opponent's position, the path of the ball, and the movement of players on the court. Most important, remember that racquetball is just a game, and one point is not worth risking your health or that of your opponent just to "make a shot."

CHAPTER 2

Introduction and Preliminaries to the Strokes in Racquetball

Being properly prepared to hit the ball is essential to the correct execution of offensive and defensive shots. This includes warming up, properly gripping the racquet, assuming the set or ready position, and pivoting to either a forehand or backhand hitting position.

GETTING READY TO PARTICIPATE: THE WARM-UP

A good rule of thumb to follow whenever beginning to exercise is "never take your body by surprise." A **warm-up** to prepare yourself mentally and physically allows your body to smoothly "shift gears" from inactivity to activity. Without a warm-up, the stress of sudden activity can cause your body to rely on reserve energy sources normally used only during emergencies. Using your reserve energy at the start of the exercise can cause you to

fatigue more quickly, and adversely affect your level of play.

The **warm-up** should consist of three phases: **relaxation, stretching,** and **increased heart activity**. Relaxation is needed to relieve internal stress. The body responds to stress by increasing muscle tension. Tight muscles work in opposition to the free and fluid movement needed for any exercise/sport activity. In addition, any stretching exercises you may do will be more effective if the muscles are first relaxed. To relax, try sitting comfortably with your eyes closed for several minutes. Concentrate only on your breathing, remembering to exhale completely.

Stretching is the second phase of the warm-up. It is important to help increase your ease and range of movement. Since racquetball is literally a game of inches, the ability to extend your reach to its limit may "make up" for slowly reacting to the ball's position. Another important function of this phase is to help alleviate

9

Getting ready to play: relaxing, stretching, increasing your heart rate.

residual soreness from previous racquetball sessions and prevent injury to tight muscles as a result of the sudden movements required by the game. All stretches should be held 15-30 seconds. Remember, do not bounce during the stretch. The last phase of the warm-up should **increase your heart rate**. This activity will also speed up the release of the body's available energy. As a result, at the beginning of the game, the reserve energy stores are not utilized. Playing racquetball will "feel" more comfortable, and you will not tire as rapidly. Stair-stepping, running in place, and rope skipping are all activities that increase your heart rate.

These three *warm-up* activities should be done in sequence immediately before entering the court to play. Many people make the mistake of warming up and then waiting for five to ten minutes before playing racquetball. Consequently, most of the effect of the warm-up is lost. The increase in heart rate will decline within one to two minutes after the warm-up is over. Therefore, no time should be wasted getting onto the court.

Last, but not least, is mental preparation for play. Unless your mind is relaxed and focused on the sport ahead, your body cannot respond properly to the challenge of the game. Concentrate on the game to be played rather than other current "events" in your life so your skills can be used to their fullest.

HOLDING THE RACQUET: THE GRIPS

The power in a racquetball stroke comes from the snap of the wrist that occurs when the ball is contacted. Unless the racquet is gripped in such a way as to maximize this snap, the potential power of a stroke will be lost. There are two basic grips that most players adapt to their style of play and a third that some use in special situations. The first, and easily the most popular, is the Eastern Forehand. The

Eastern Forehand, as its name implies, is used to hit only shots on the racquet-hand (forehand) side of the body. Its counterpart on the non-racquet-hand side is the Eastern Backhand and will be discussed later.

Eastern Forehand Grip

The easiest way to assume an **Eastern Forehand** grip is merely to hold the racquet on edge so that it is perpendicular to the floor and then "shake hands" with the handle. In the shaking hands position, the first finger and thumb of the racquet hand should form a "V" along the top of the handle, the point of the "V" lying on the midline of the handle's surface. The fingers are spread in a "trigger" position to allow for better wrist snap.

Another way to assume this position is to hold the racquet in the non-racquet hand so that the racquet is again on edge. Place your racquet hand with fingers spread on the strings of the racquet so that the palm is flat against the racquet face. Slide your racquet hand down the racquet until the end of the handle meets the end of your palm, and wrap your fingers

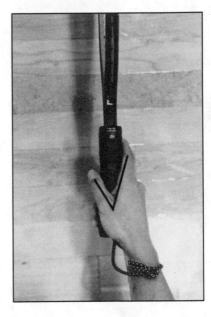

Eastern Forehand Grip.

around the handle. Again you should check to see if the "V" formed by your first finger and thumb is pointed properly along the top surface of the handle. Be careful not to grip the racquet so that the handle lies perpendicular to your fingers in a "fist" grip or the wrist snap will be lost. If you turn the racquet over so that your palm is pointed toward the ceiling of

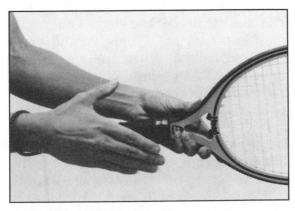

Shaking hands with the racquet.

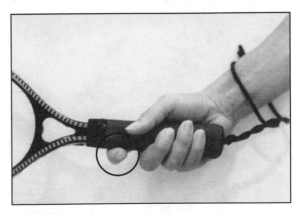

Trigger Grip.

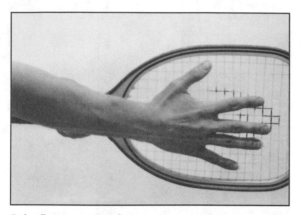

Palm flat on racquet face.

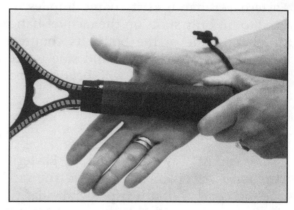

Handle of racquet lies diagonally across palm of hand.

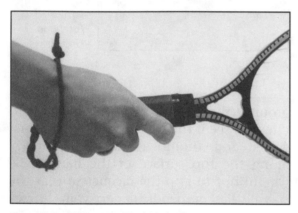

Assuming the Eastern Forehand grip.

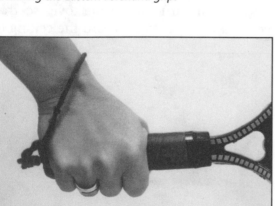

Improper grip on racquet, fingers perpendicular to handle.

the court and open your hand, a racquet in the correct position should lie diagonally across the palm. The handle should cover the first knuckle of the first finger and the bottom left side of the palm.

Eastern Backhand Grip

If you use this grip for your forehand shots, you must change your grip to hit backhand shots (shots to the non-racquet-hand side). This is due to the way in which the arm moves about the elbow. The construction of the elbow joint causes the forearm to move only up and down (flex and extend) when the arm is held straight at your side. When hitting a backhand shot, the racquet arm is pulled across the body and then extended. If the racquet is held with the forehand grip, the racquet head will be turned up when the ball is hit. Thus, shots that should be hit straight into the front wall will be "popped," or hit up toward the ceiling. To hit a level backhand shot, you must change your grip from the **Eastern Forehand** to the **Eastern Backhand** grip. To find this position on your racquet, assume the forehand grip just discussed and hold the racquet on edge. With your non-racquet hand, turn the top of the racquet clockwise toward the fingers of your gripping hand so that the forefinger-thumb "V" falls on the top left bevel of the racquet. This grip rotates the head of the racquet downward to compensate for the elbow's inability to rotate and allows you to hit a level ball.

The problem with changing from the forehand to the backhand grip is that it takes TIME. Thus, it is important that you immediately recognize when a backhand shot should be hit to give you as much time as possible to make the switch. A similar problem occurs after the backhand shot is taken. The grip must be changed back to the forehand placement. Unfortunately, many players have difficulty changing grips and hitting the ball too! But a player must do something to change the angle of the racquet head!

One alternative solution to this problem is to simply rotate the wrist forward when hitting a backhand shot. This turns the racquet head downward and allows a flat shot to be hit. Returning to the Eastern Forehand grip only takes a "twist" of the wrist. The major problem with this method is that it is so easy, new players often FORGET to do it!

Either way of changing the racquet position for a backhand can be effective as long as you consistently use it. Choose one method and practice it all the time.

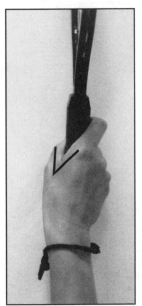

The change to the
Eastern Backhand Grip.

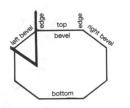

"V" for Eastern Backhand Grip.

Continental Grip

A second alternative to changing grips is to avoid using the Eastern Forehand and Backhand grips completely. Instead, use the **Continental grip**. In the **Continental grip**, the racquet is held in a position midway between the Eastern Forehand and Backhand. To assume this grip, the racquet must be rotated clockwise one-eighth of a turn from the Eastern Forehand grip. Now the "V" will point to the top left edge of the handle. Thus, with the Continental grip, little or no adjustment must be made for either a forehand or backhand shot, although the wrist may be slightly rotated clockwise to adjust the face of the racquet during a backhand shot to hit a level ball.

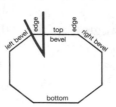

"V" for Continental Grip.

Continental Grip.

Western Grip.

Western Grip

The third grip is called the **Western** grip or "frying pan" grip. It is similar to the grip you use on a frying pan handle when you lift the pan off a stove or pick your racquet up off the floor. This grip is preferred by some players for overhead forehand shots. However, it is not necessary to change to this grip at all.

After hitting a few balls, always recheck your grip to make sure that the racquet has not twisted in your hand. Some players will even mark the "V" placement of the thumb and forefinger on the racquet's top bevel with tape. This helps to guide the correct hand positioning.

Eastern Forehand Grip marked with a "V" on the racquet.

Points to Remember

1. Note the position of the "V" on the racquet handle and make sure that it matches your hand placement.

2. Keep your fingers spread out in a pistol or trigger finger grip — do not keep a fist grip on the handle.

3. Change to a backhand grip or compensate for the elbow's movement by rotating the wrist to hit a ball on the non-racquet side. Change back to a forehand grip after the shot has been taken.

4. Overhead shots may be hit using a Western grip.

5. Continental grip may be used to hit all balls.

SET, PIVOT, AND STROKE

The Set

The **set** or "ready" position prepares you to hit the ball. Begin each stroke at the set position and return to it following each hit. The set position allows you to move quickly to hit a ball with either your forehand or backhand.

To get in the **set** position, stand with your feet shoulder width apart, toes pointing forward and weight equally balanced on the balls of the feet. The racquet

Set position — front view.

Set position — side view.

should be held in front of you at waist height, and a forehand grip should be used. Your non-racquet hand should be free to provide ease of movement. Knees should be slightly bent and pointed forward. Shoulders, head, and neck are relaxed, with your eyes free to follow the movement of the ball. Breathing must be deep and regular.

Points to Remember

1. Face the front wall, with toes pointed forward.
2. Weight is equally balanced on the balls of the feet, which are placed shoulder width apart.
3. Hold the racquet with a forehand grip at waist height in front of you.
4. Knees are bent; head, shoulders, neck relaxed, and the body is ready to "spring" into action.

The Pivot

As soon as you have decided if the ball is to be hit with a forehand or backhand stroke, you must **pivot** or turn your body to prepare for the hit. The sooner the decision can be made, the better prepared you will be to hit the ball. So decide **quickly**. The importance of the pivot is that it turns the hips sideways to the front wall. This allows for the player to "step into" the ball and add his/her body weight into the power of the stroke. A baseball batter will take the same position. Except to bunt, the batter will always stand sideways to the pitcher and step into the pitch by shifting his weight forward. Thus, the ball

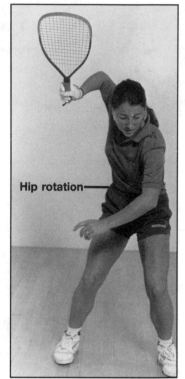

Hip rotation

Pivot position for forehand stroke.

Weight shift

Wrist cock

Shifting weight into the ball from a pivot position.

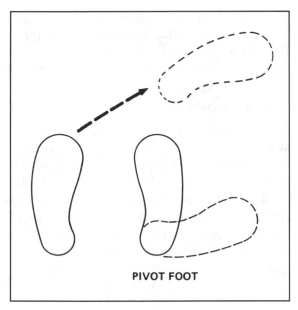

Forward pivot.

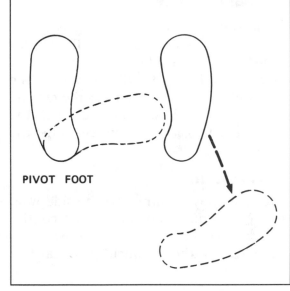

Backstep pivot.

can be hit with more force. Similarly, the pivot in racquetball positions you to step into the ball, shift your weight, and increase the power of your stroke. This is especially important for women players who may have weak arms and wrists.

The pivot may be done by moving either forward or back. In either case, you must shift your weight to one foot to turn to face a side wall. Your free foot will either be pulled forward or behind you to complete the pivot. Your body should finish the pivot with your hips facing a side wall. Whether you pivot and step forward or backward depends on where the ball rebounds and whether you have to move up or back to reach it. Further adjustments in body position can be made by "cross-stepping" forward or backward.

During any pivot motion, your eyes must not lose contact with the ball, and your face should be directed toward the ball.

Points to Remember

1. Decide quickly where the ball is to be hit, and pivot to that side immediately.
2. After the pivot, the body should face a side wall.
3. Move either forward or backward to the ball by cross-stepping up or back.
4. Keep your eyes and face directed at the ball.

Forehand Stroke

The only problem remaining is to hit the ball! Forehand strokes will be discussed first, then additional information on backhand strokes will be given. The forehand stroke itself begins as the racquet is carried from the set stance through the position change that results from the pivot.

BACKSWING

As the body is turned to the side wall, so is the racquet. But the racquet continues to be pulled back so that with the elbow bent, the racquet is in a line between your body and the back wall. This is called the **backswing**. In this position, the racquet is held almost at right angles to the forearm, which serves to "cock" the wrist.

WRIST COCK

The **wrist cock** is a critical part of your stroke. It is the "uncocking" or snapping of the wrist and racquet at the ball which generates the speed and power of the stroke. Without cocking the wrist, as in pulling the hammer back in a gun, there would be no way of hitting the ball with explosive force. To be most effective, the snap or "uncocking" of the wrist must occur when the ball is contacted.

Completed backswing with racquet in line between the back wall and the body.

Wrist cock on the backswing.

FORWARD SWING

As you prepare to swing the racquet forward, you must first shift your weight forward. This is done by stepping into the path of the ball with the foot closest to the front wall. It is important that during the swing, the elbow remain close to the side of the body. This position enables the ball to be contacted below waist level and prevents "over-the-shoulder" shots. The racquet hand should lead the racquet through the swing. This position helps to maintain a "cocked" wrist during the swing. The elbow should remain bent until the ball is contacted. At that point, the elbow is extended and the arm straightened. Once the arm is extended, the racquet should be at the same level off the floor as your hand, with the head perpendicular to the floor, or "on edge."

Forward swing maintaining wrist cock.

Points to Remember

1. On the backswing, pull the racquet back with elbow bent to a point directly behind you in line with your body and the back wall.

2. Hold the racquet almost at a right angle to the forearm to "cock" the wrist.

3. On the forward swing, shift weight to your forward foot.

4. Keep the elbow bent on the forward swing, hold the upper arm close to the body.

5. Maintain wrist cock through the swing, with the racquet head trailing the wrist and elbow through the swing.

6. At the point of contact, extend the arm and keep the racquet head perpendicular to the floor, at the same level as the hand.

CONTACT

Contact with the ball should be made slightly behind the forward foot as your weight is shifted forward. At the point of impact, the wrist is snapped. Contact with the ball should be made as close to the ground as possible, with your arm extended. To do this, you must bend your knees to drop your waist and racquet close to the ground. Do not drop the racquet below the level of the hand to hit a low ball. Your whole body must lower to insure that the racquet head remains on edge and perpendicular to the ground.

Weight shifted forward to contact ball.

the ball rebounds off the floor and bounces toward your racquet; and (3) after the ball reaches the height of its bounce and is falling back to the floor and below your waist. For experienced players, hitting the ball as it rebounds off the floor (2) maintains a fast tempo in the game. The beginning player, however, should wait for the ball to reach the height of its bounce and begin to fall back to the floor for the second time (3) before hitting the ball.

Points to Remember

1. Shift your weight onto your forward foot during the forward swing.

2. Hit the ball slightly behind your forward foot.

3. At the point of impact, snap the wrist and extend the arm.

4. If possible, contact the ball low to the ground, by bending and lowering your body to the ball.

The ball can be contacted at one of three points during its flight: (1) as it rebounds off the front wall, dropping below your waist toward the floor; (2) after

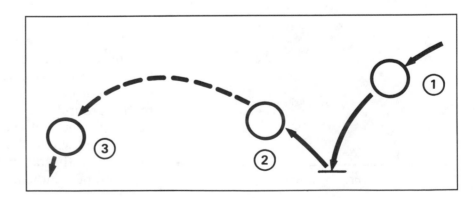

Points of contact for a rebounding ball.

FOLLOW-THROUGH

A mistake that many beginners make is failing to complete the stroke, or to **follow-through** after the hit is made. Consequently, these players "punch" at the ball with shortened stroke and lose the force of their hit. The **follow-through** made after contact with the ball allows for the completion of the stroke and hitting the ball with all the force of your swing. It also allows you to recover from the stroke quickly and adjust your stance back to the set position to await your next hit.

In general, a racquetball stroke should end with the racquet swung past the midline of the body and finish high off the non-racquet side. The follow-through should rotate the shoulders and hips so that they are again facing the front wall, with the front foot acting as a pivot. At the end of the stroke, your weight should be concentrated on your forward foot but balanced so that you do not fall down. During this follow-through, the body should be kept low to the ground. Standing up too quickly will cause the ball to be "carried" upward with your movement and make it difficult for you to hit low balls.

Follow-through of the forehand stroke.

High follow through

Weight forward

> ## Points to Remember
>
> 1. Finish the stroke with the racquet swung past the midline of the body.
> 2. Stay low; but allow high racquet follow-through.
> 3. After the ball has been contacted, allow the body to rotate toward the front wall following the direction of the arm swing.
> 4. Don't stand up until the follow-through is complete.

Backhand Stroke

To hit a **backhand stroke**, use either a backhand grip on the racquet, or turn the racquet face down by rotating the wrist forward. The movement begins as the forehand stroke from the set position. The pivot, however, results in the player facing the opposite side wall. Again, the pivot can be made either by stepping forward or backward, depending on the position of the ball (see page 17). After pivoting, the hips should be parallel to the side wall.

Set position before backhand.

Shoulder turn

Hip rotation

Backhand pivot.

BACKSWING

The backhand stroke is begun by pulling the racquet across the body with the **backswing**. At the end of the **backswing**, the racquet is held in line between your shoulder and the back wall with the elbow bent. In this position, the upper body must rotate more than in the forehand stroke in order for the racquet to be positioned behind the shoulder. When correctly rotated, the chin should almost rest on the shoulder of the racquet arm.

Hip rotation

Backswing position for backhand stroke.

WRIST COCK

The racquet must be held with the **wrist cocked**, as in the forehand stroke. In the

Wrist cock.

Forward swing with the racquet trailing the hand.

cocked position, the racquet is almost at a 90-degree angle to the forearm.

FORWARD SWING

As the **forward swing** is begun, the player's weight is shifted to the front foot. The racquet head should trail the elbow and the hand during the forward swing to maintain the cocked position. The bent elbow should be held close to the body and used as an axis to pivot the racquet around. In error, a beginning player often pulls the elbow out in front of the body towards the front wall. When this happens, the racquet head is pulled across the body rather than swung around, power is lost and the ball is rebounded to the side of the court.

Points to Remember

1. Use a backhand grip, or rotate your wrist forward to change the position of the racquet head to hit the ball.
2. Pivot to the opposite side wall from that turned to with the forehand stroke.
3. Pull the racquet back to a position between the shoulder and the back wall with the elbow bent.
4. Cock the wrist at the end of the backswing.
5. On the forward swing, keep your elbow close to the body and pivot around it.
6. Keep the racquet head behind the hand on the forward swing to maintain the wrist cock.

CONTACT

To **contact** the ball, your weight should be forward on the front foot. Extend the elbow at the point of contact so that the racquet head is now in line with the wrist and elbow. The racquet should contact the ball just inside of the forward foot as low to the ground as possible. When the ball is contacted, the wrist is snapped sharply to increase the impact on the ball.

Contacting the ball.

Points to Remember

1. Your weight is shifted forward at contact with the ball.
2. Hit the ball when it is just inside of your forward foot and close to the ground.
3. At the point of contact, extend the arm, keeping the elbow close to the body.
4. As the racquet hits the ball, snap the wrist to increase the power in your stroke.

FOLLOW-THROUGH

As with the forehand, the backhand stroke is finished with a **follow-through**. With the **follow-through**, the chest and hips end up facing the front wall, and the racquet is swung to a point opposite the shoulder of the racquet arm. Without a follow-through, the strength of the swing is lost. Until the stroke is complete, keep your head down to prevent yourself from standing up before the ball leaves the racquet. Otherwise the ball will be lifted up with your movement.

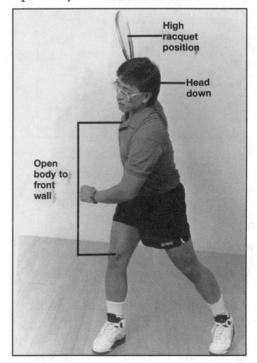

Follow-through.

Points to Remember

1. Finish the stroke with a follow-through so the racquet stops at a point opposite the forward shoulder.
2. Stay low after hitting the ball.

The success of either a forehand or backhand stroke is dependent upon your ability to hit the ball consistently with the same stroking motion. This means that the point of contact with the ball in relation to your body must not vary. The only way to assure this is to **MOVE** on the court so that the ball is aligned properly with your stroke. Too many beginning players (and some better ones, too!) are content to hit the ball regardless of where it is, if it is within their reach. This tactic results in many unorthodox strokes in an attempt to hit the ball. Since most of these shots have never been practiced, these strokes merely rebound the ball back to the front wall rather than being accurately placed. It is the player that is consistently positioned to hit a practiced shot that can make conscious changes in the racquet head angle or force of impact to **DIRECT** the ball away from the opponent's reach. Now *THAT* is racquetball!

COMMON ERRORS AND HOW TO CORRECT THEM

1. I never know where the ball is going.

   A. You fail to position yourself so that the ball is contacted at the same place in relation to your body at all times. Move in the court, and go to where the ball will be. Set yourself up, and hit the ball as you have practiced.

2. I can't hit the ball hard.

   A. Check to see if you are following through rather than just "punching" at the ball and stopping your arm motion.

   B. Make sure that you are snapping your wrist at the moment of contact with the ball to increase the impact.

   C. Check to make sure that you are hitting the ball when your weight is shifted forward.

3. The ball always goes "up." I can't seem to hit a low ball.

   A. Check your grip to see if the racquet head is pointed up at contact.

   B. Watch your body position to see if you are standing up before the ball leaves the racquet head. You may be "carrying" the ball up with you.

   C. Emphasize a low follow-through rather than just punching at the ball.

   D. Let the ball drop lower before you hit it and keep the racquet perpendicular to the floor.

   (continued)

4. I miss the ball completely or the ball always hits a side wall first.

   A. You are probably hitting the ball off of your back foot. This area is not in your field of vision, and you lose track of the ball. Hitting the ball from this position also means that your arm has not swung the racquet far enough so the racquet head is parallel to the front wall at contact. Instead, the racquet head is still angled toward a side wall, causing the ball to rebound in that direction.

5. I hit the ball into the side wall.

   A. Usually this means that you have not changed from the set position to the pivot. Your hips are therefore facing the front wall rather than the side wall. As a result, your stroke comes across the body and directs the ball into the side wall.

   B. If it is a backhand shot, you may also be pulling your elbow in front of your body rather than pivoting around it during the swing.

   C. You could be hitting off your back foot. See answer 4A.

6. I can't hit my backhand with strength and power.

   A. You are positioning yourself too close to the ball on your backhand side. As a result, you cannot extend your arm and utilize the wrist snap at the point of contact to maximize your power.

CHAPTER 3

Offensive Strokes

An **offensive shot** is designed to win a point outright by virtue of the skill with which it is hit. Regardless of where your opponent is playing, the well-executed offensive shot should always be a winner. Several basic offensive shots exist. Any offensive shot may be hit with either a forehand or backhand stroke, and the skilled player can use either stroke with equal effectiveness.

The beginning player will usually choose to hit an offensive shot from the forehand side. This gives credence to the observation of a player having a "weak" side, i.e., one from which an offensive shot is usually not hit (in most cases the backhand). Therefore, a good strategy to follow when playing a *"weak"-sided* opponent is to hit your offensive shots so that they must be returned with a "weak" side shot (i.e., backhand). With this strategy, if your offensive shot is not "perfect," you are usually not setting up an offensive return.

The type of offensive shot you hit is dependent upon your skill with each shot,

your position on the court, and in a few instances, your opponent's court position. To hit accurate offensive shots requires hours of practice on the court. Therefore, you should not rely on offensive shots in a game situation until you can hit them consistently in practice.

KILL SHOTS

A **kill shot** is the ultimate offensive weapon of a racquetball player. By definition, a kill shot is a ball that hits the front wall so low and hard that the rebound to the floor occurs almost simultaneously with the front-wall hit. This rebound makes it virtually impossible for your opponent to return the ball even if he/she is standing in the ball's path.

All kill shots, except the overhead kill, should be hit when the ball is close to the floor. Contact with the ball must be made by bending your knees to drop your waist and racquet arm close to the floor. Ideally, the ball should be struck when it is positioned between your bent knee and the

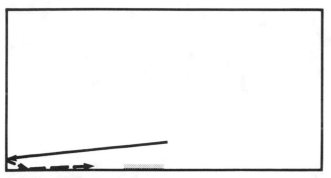

Rebound of a kill shot off the front wall.

1

top of your foot. The shot is then made with a normal forehand or backhand motion, with emphasis on generating power in the hit by stepping into the ball and using a good wrist snap. The harder the ball is hit, the farther away from the front wall a kill shot can be successfully made. Most beginners, however, because of their weaker stroke, should concentrate on hitting kill shots from a mid-court position or just behind the short line.

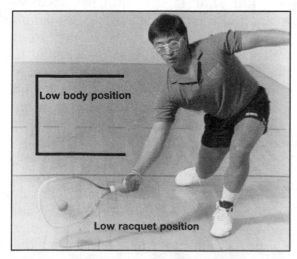

Racquet position off the court to hit a kill shot.

1

2 — Lowering body position / Weight shift

3 — Head down / Legs bent / Low racquet position perpendicular to floor

4 — High racquet / Staying low

5 — High racquet / Still low, but coming up

Forehand kill shot sequence.

2 — Eyes focused on ball / Weight shift / Lowering body

3 — Head down eyes on ball / Wrist cocked / Legs bent

4 — Head stays down / Staying low / Low racquet position perpendicular to floor

5 — High follow-through / Still low, but coming up

Backhand kill shot sequence.

The critical factor in hitting a good kill shot is keeping the racquet perpendicular to the floor and the swing parallel to the floor to insure hitting a flat or level ball. A level hit will rebound off the front wall at or below the height that it hits into the wall. Thus, a low, level ball hit to the front wall has the greatest potential for achieving the desired kill shot effect.

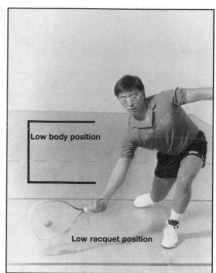

Head-on view of kill shot.

Front Wall-Straight-In Kill Shot

A **front wall-straight-in kill** shot hits the front wall first and rebounds toward the back wall without touching a side wall. This shot can be hit from anyplace in the court and at anytime during play, but it is most effective if your opponent is next to (A) or behind you (B) in the court. Ideally, this kill shot should be directed toward the half of the front wall farthest away from the opposing player. Since the ball follows a straight path to the front wall, the racquet face must be parallel to this surface when it strikes the ball. In addition, keeping the swing level to the floor will insure that the ball is hit low to the front wall.

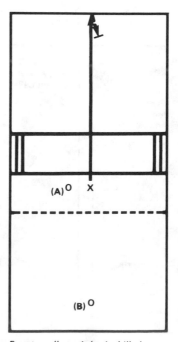

Front wall straight-in kill shot.

Front Wall-Side Wall Kill (Corner)

If the opponent is in the back court (B) or close to a side wall (A), a **corner kill** may be used. In this shot, the racquet is held so that the face is aimed at a corner of the front wall. As a result, the ball will hit the front wall close to a front wall-side wall crotch and quickly rebound to the nearest side wall. Depending upon the angle with which the ball is hit, the ball may bounce toward a front or mid-court position. The success of this shot depends on your opponent's court position and how accurately you can hit the ball. If the ball is not hit low as a kill shot should be, or if the opponent is not far enough in the back court or toward a side wall, the shot will be a setup for an easy return to the front wall. One way to adjust for a quick-reacting opponent who covers the court well is to hit the corner kill at a sharper

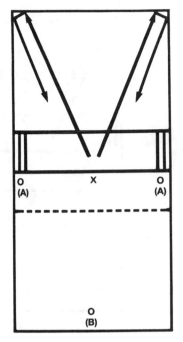

Front wall - Side wall kill (corner).

Racquet head angled to front corner for kill shot.

angle closer to the corner so that the ball rebounds toward the front-court position.

Side Wall-Front Wall (Pinch Kill)

The **pinch kill shot** hits one side wall before rebounding into the front wall. An advantage of hitting the **pinch kill** rather than the corner kill is simply the placement of the rebounding ball. Where the corner kill is more likely to rebound close to a mid-court position, the pinch kill rebounds tightly into a front corner. However, to be most effective with the pinch kill, the opponent should be next to or behind you in the court. Whether the shot is directed to the left or right front corner

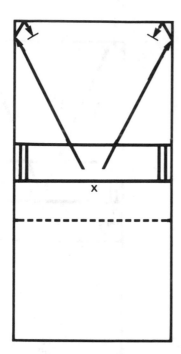

*Side wall - Front
wall kill (pinch).*

Pinch kill.

depends partly on your position in the court, but more importantly on your opponent's position. Ideally, you should always hit the ball so that the rebound off the front wall is traveling away from the opponent. If this can't be done, then at least hit the ball so that it rebounds toward the opponent's weak side. A shot to the weak side, even if not perfectly hit, should not result in an offensive return.

To hit a pinch kill (as with the corner kill), the racquet face upcn contact with the ball must be angled to the side wall rather than held parallel to the front wall. The ball must be contacted close to the ground. To do this, bend your knees, drop your waist, and extend your racquet arm

down. In all other respects, the technique for hitting this kill shot is similar to that for a forehand or backhand stroke.

The pinch kill is ideal for the beginning player because he/she can make a mistake in hitting this shot and still score a point. Since the rebound is to a front court position, even a ball hit too high or one that rebounds off the floor may be impossible for your opponent to reach as long as he/she is in the back court.

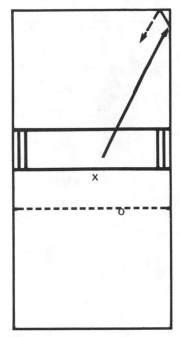

Pinch kill hit to opponent's backhand.

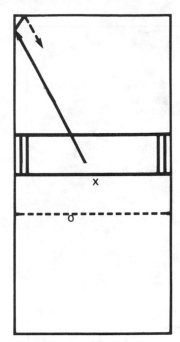

Pinch kill hit away from opponent.

Overhead Kill

The **overhead kill shot** is popular with beginning players but falls out of favor as the player develops other offensive weapons. The object of the overhead kill is the same as for any kill shot, but the stroking technique is different. This kill shot is hit off a ball that is above shoulder level rather than close to the ground. It is hit from the forehand side with much the same motion used in a tennis serve. The stroke is begun by pivoting and pulling the racquet back as if to hit a forehand stroke. However, as the forward swing is begun, the racquet is lifted in a circular motion as if you were going to throw it to the front wall. The chest and hips are rotated to face the front wall as you step forward to hit the ball. The ball is con-

tacted just in front of the forward foot with an extended arm. At contact, the face of the racquet should be angled slightly down to the front wall. To assume this position, a Western grip is preferred over any other forehand grip to turn the face of the racquet. To maximize the power of the stroke, the ball should always be hit with the arm in an extended position with a downward wrist snap (4). Complete the stroke with a follow-through, dropping the racquet across the body. Ideally, the ball should be directed low into the front corner of the court. To have the best chance of success, the overhead kill should hit a side wall as well as the front wall to deaden the rebound of the ball. Otherwise, if not hit perfectly, the ball will rebound high into the air at the same angle at which it hit the wall. The high bounce gives even a slow opponent adequate time to position him/herself for the return. Consequently, the overhead kill is considered a "low-percentage" shot because it is hard to score a point off a ball that is not hit perfectly. Therefore, beginning players are advised to be patient and wait for the ball to drop below waist level rather than hit an overhead kill. Then, a corner or pinch kill can be hit. Both of these kill shots are more difficult to return than the overhead kill, even if all shots are hit incorrectly.

High racquet position

1

Arm extended

Weight shift

2

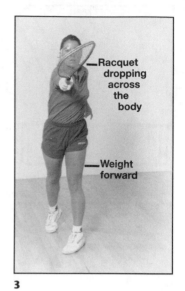

Racquet dropping across the body

Weight forward

3

Completion of follow through

Weight forward

4

5

Sequence of overhead kill shot.

Rebound of poorly hit overhead kill bouncing high off the floor.

Points to Remember:

1. To hit an effective kill shot, wait for the ball to fall low to the ground — at least below your knee.
2. To reach the ball, pivot, bend your knees and drop your waist to lower your racquet arm toward the ground.
3. To hit a straight-in kill shot, keep your racquet face perpendicular to the floor, and parallel to the front wall. Swing level with the floor using a good wrist snap.
4. To direct a kill shot to a front corner, you must angle your racquet face to the corner that you wish to hit.
5. Try to angle your kill shot away from your opponent's court position or hit to his/her weak-side to insure a successful shot.

PASSING SHOTS

A **passing shot**, unlike the kill shot, requires no new techniques to master. Its effectiveness depends only on your opponent's court position and your ability to place the ball. The passing shot, as its name implies, is a ball that literally goes "past" the opponent. Therefore, it is most advantageous to hit when the opposing player is in the front-, mid-, or center court areas. In this way, the ball can go "past" the opponent and "beat" him/her into the back court. If hit low off the front wall, a passing shot will die in the back court and not rebound into a center court position. Without rebounding hard off the back wall, the ball in essence is "out-of-play" except to a heroic effort. At the very least, if the ball is returned, it will usually be a desperation shot that you can return for a winner or at least

will push your opponent to use up his/her energy reserves.

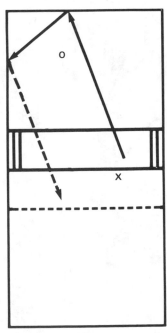

Passing shot hit to opponent in front court.

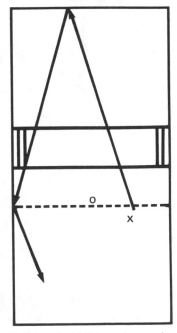

Passing shot hit to opponent in center court.

The most critical error made by beginning players when using a passing shot is hitting the ball with too much force. As a result, instead of dying in the back court, the ball rebounds off the back wall into play and negates the advantage that the passing shot offers.

The passing shot can be hit with either a forehand, backhand, or overhead stroke. The ball should be directed to hit the front wall at a point between waist and knee height off the floor. In all cases, however, the lower the rebound off the front wall, the less chance that a return will be made. The ball can either be hit directly to a back corner or angled to rebound from the front wall to contact a side wall on the way to the back court. If the ball is angled toward a side wall, it should hit either at the same distance or farther from the front

wall as your opponent is standing. This will help not only to slow the movement of the ball into the back court but discourage your opponent from trying to hit the ball as it rebounds off the front wall because it will be out of reach. Should the ball hit the side wall in front of your opponent's court position, it will pass through the center court and allow your opponent to make a play on the ball.

Two types of passing shots are common — the down-the-line pass and the cross-court pass.

Down-The-Line Pass

The **down-the-line pass** could really be called the down-the-wall (wallpaper) pass. This ball is hit so that it travels in a line along the side wall, 1 to 3 feet from it and below waist level. As stated before, hitting the ball too hard will cause a strong rebound off the back wall and possibly

Passing shot hitting the side wall at the same distance from the front wall that the opponent is standing.

Down-the-line pass.

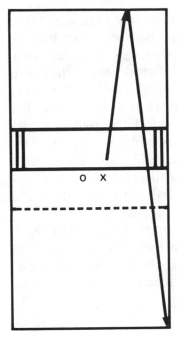

Down-the-line pass.

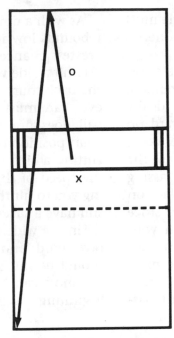

Passing shot when opponent is in front court, to weak side.

Cross-Court Pass

The **cross-court pass** moves the ball from one side of the court to the other in order to "pass" the opponent. It does this by following the path of a "V" across the court. Depending upon where you are positioned in the court, the ball will rebound off the front wall close to its center. You must experiment with the exact placement of the ball as you hit from different court positions. What will always be true is that the ball will rebound from the front wall at an angle equal to the angle of impact. To prevent the opponent from hitting the

allow a return to be made. This passing shot is ideally hit when you are between your opponent and the side wall down which you are hitting or when the opposing player is "caught" in a front court position. In either case, hit the ball toward the side wall that is the farthest distance from your opponent. If he/she is playing a center court position, hit to the backhand side. A forehand stroke should be used to hit passing shots to the forehand side of the court and a backhand stroke for balls directed to the backhand side.

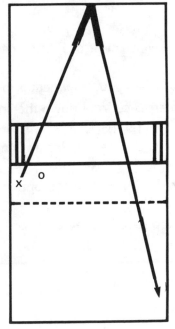

Cross-court passing shot with opponent close to side wall.

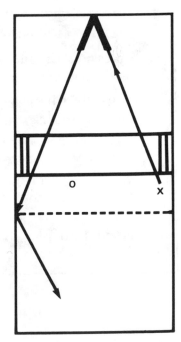

Cross-court passing shot with opponent in center court.

rebound off the front wall, this angle must be large enough to avoid the opponent's reach.

As with a down-the-line pass, the cross-court shot may be hit with a forehand, backhand, or overhead stroke. It is ideally used when your opponent is forward on your side of the court, is in a center court position, or is positioned closer to the front wall. One advantage of the passing shot is that it can be hit from anyplace on the court, including the back court, since the success of the shot depends on your opponent's court position. It is an easy shot to learn and win with because most right-handed players can use their stronger forehands to hit cross-court passing shots to their opponent's weaker backhands.

As with a down-the-line pass, a ball that rebounds low into the back court has the greatest chance of success. This ball may also hit a side wall before rebounding into the back court area. As stated earlier, however, care must be taken to insure that the ball does not rebound through a center court position or in front of the opponent. Hitting a side wall will also help to slow the speed of the ball on the court, allowing you to hit the ball with more force and still have a successful passing shot.

Since a wide margin of error exists with how hard and at what angle the ball should be hit, successful cross-court passing shots can be made by even the most beginning player.

Points to Remember:

1. A passing shot can be hit with any stroke. Its success is dependent upon your opponent's court position.

2. Do not use a passing shot when your opponent is in a back court position.

3. A passing shot can be hit cross-court or down-the-line from anyplace on the court.

4. As long as the ball goes into the back court, the lower the passing shot rebounds off the front wall, the greater its chance of being a winning shot.

5. The passing shot may hit a side wall after rebounding from the front wall, but it should not be angled to hit in front of the opponent or to go through the center court area.

6. Hitting the passing shot too hard will cause the ball to rebound off the back wall into play.

COMMON ERRORS AND HOW TO CORRECT THEM

1. My kill shots always hit the floor before they reach the front wall.

   A. Usually you have angled the racquet face down at the point of impact with the ball, thus driving the ball into the ground. Concentrate on keeping your racquet face perpendicular to the floor and the stroke parallel to the floor.

2. My kill shots are never low enough to the front wall.

   A. Be patient and wait for the ball to drop closer to the ground before hitting it. This means that you will have to bend your knees and lower your waist to drop your racquet to the ball. Try to make contact with the ball just off the tops of your shoes. If this does not help, you may be scooping at the ball with the racquet and hitting it on the upswing, which lifts the ball to the front wall higher than you want it to hit. A level swing with the floor will correct this problem.

3. I hit my cross-court shots right back to my opponent because the ball bounces off a side wall into the center court.

   A. Take some angle off your hit and aim more for the center of the front wall.

4. My down-the-line passing shot always hits the side wall.

   A. You racquet head is not parallel to the front wall when you contact the ball, but is angled toward the side wall that you are hitting. Snap the wrist and swing through the ball. Also, check to make sure that you are contacting the ball off your forward foot. Contacting the ball off your back foot can cause the ball to rebound into the side wall after hitting the front wall.

5. My overhead kill shot hits (a) the floor first or (b) too high off the front wall.

   A. (a) When the floor is hit first, either the ball is hit when it is too far in front of you or when your wrist is bent too much, causing the racquet head to be angled to the floor. Check the position of your body relative to the ball when you hit the overhead, and hold the racquet so that it appears to be an extension of you arm.

   (b) Hitting the ball too high off the front wall usually results from hitting the ball too far behind your front foot or even over your head, which prohibits you from angling the hit downward. Again, check the position of the ball when you make contact, and be sure that the contact point is in front of your forward foot.

6. My passing shots always rebound off the back wall into a center court position.

   A. Take some of the force off your stroke, and hit the ball lower off the front wall to insure a shorter rebound from the back. If this does not help, try to hit a side wall to deaden the ball's movement.

CHAPTER 4

Defensive Strokes

Rather than scoring a point, the purpose of a **defensive shot** is to PREVENT your opponent from hitting a winning shot. This goal can be achieved only if the ball rebounds high off the front wall, preventing a kill-shot return, or rebounds to a court position that does not favor an offensive return. Ideally, the best defensive shot is hit in such a way as to have the ball rebound from the front wall high into the back court and close to the side wall. Several strokes accomplish this purpose, at least one of which should immediately become part of your repertoire of shots.

CEILING SHOTS

Front Wall-Ceiling

The **ceiling shot** can be hit with a forehand or backhand stroke off a ball that falls below waist level or with an overhead stroke on a high ball. A front wall-to-ceiling shot hits the front wall before the ceiling. Upon contact with the front wall, the ball rebounds to the ceiling close to the front wall-ceiling crotch and then is directed downward to bounce on the floor just past the short line. If hit with enough force, the rebound of the ball off the floor

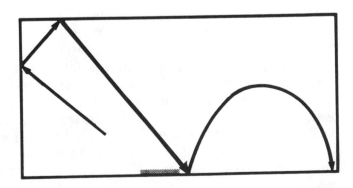

Front wall - Ceiling shot.

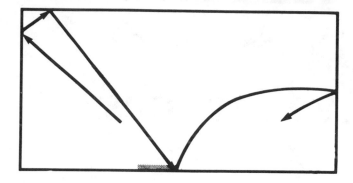

Front wall - Ceiling hit with too much force and rebounding off the back wall.

will carry the ball high over the head of the opponent and into a back corner. Since the ball must be returned before striking the floor twice, your opponent must hit the ball from this corner position without the benefit of a rebound off the floor. Thus, this court position makes it difficult to hit an offensive shot because of the ball's proximity to the walls. However, the harder you hit the front wall-ceiling shot, the higher the height of the bounce off the floor and the greater the chance the ball will hit and rebound off the back wall with enough force to provide room to hit the ball before it touches the floor a second time. Therefore, care must be taken to hit the ball with adequate force to provide a high bounce to force the opponent to the back corner but not so hard as to cause a rebound off the back wall into a center-court position.

The front wall-ceiling shot hit from a ball that has dropped below waist level begins as any other forehand or backhand stroke. The pivot to the side wall is followed by the backswing with the wrist cocked. However, as the forward swing is begun, the racquet head must be turned back, or "opened," toward the ceiling. This racquet face position directs the ball toward the top of the front wall.

Open racquet for ceiling shot.

The front wall-ceiling shot hit with an overhead stroke, whether from the forehand or backhand side, is similar in technique to an overhead kill shot (see page 33). Like the kill shot, contact with the ball is made just off the forward foot, with the hips and chest facing the front wall and the arm extended. A Western grip is preferred by many players, since it opens the face of the racquet to the ceiling. The difference between the ceiling shot and the offensive kill return is the angle of the racquet face when the ball is contacted.

Ceiling shot sequence.

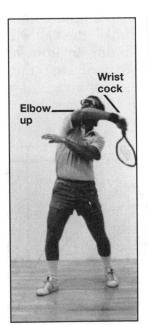

Backhand overhead ceiling shot.

With the ceiling shot, the face must be angled toward the top of the front wall. To do this, the wrist cannot be snapped from its laid-back position on the forward swing. This will keep the racquet directed upward. The stroke should finish with a follow-through to insure hitting the ball with power.

Laid back racquet for overhead ceiling shot.

A front wall-ceiling shot is most effective if hit when your opponent is already in the back court. Since the ball strikes the floor close to the short line, if your opponent is playing nearby, he/she may be tempted to hit the ball immediately after the bounce. A back-court position would not result in the same

temptation, and the desired effect of the ceiling shot can be achieved.

To insure the most difficult return possible, the front wall-ceiling shot should be directed to "run" along a side wall before it bounces into the back corner. If in addition the ball is directed to your opponent's backhand side, this defensive shot may not only result in a weak return but possibly no return at all. Thus, this defensive shot may actually score a point for you.

Ceiling-Front Wall Shot

A **ceiling-front wall shot** is a variation of the **front wall-ceiling shot** in that the ball hits both surfaces but in the reverse order. Although both are ceiling shots and hit with a similar technique, this ceiling shot is hit with a racquet that is angled more toward the ceiling. The ball should be directed to hit the ceiling approximately 2 to 3 feet from the ceiling-front wall crotch. With this stroke, the ball will rebound to the floor, hitting in front of the service zone before bouncing into the back-court area. The advantage of a ceiling-front wall shot is that it can be an

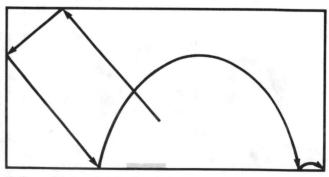

Ceiling - front wall defensive shot.

effective defensive shot even if your opponent is near center court. The ball rebounds to the floor in front of the service line, which means that your opponent must retreat to the back court to await the fall of the ball. Thus, with this shot the opponent will be forced into a poor court position. In all other respects, the strategic use of a ceiling-front wall shot is the same as for a front wall-ceiling shot: (1) keep the ball in play; (2) move your opponent to a back-court position; and (3) force a return that is not an offensive shot.

Either ceiling shot can be hit from any part of the court and should be practiced from all court positions. If you are standing to one side of center, you can hit the shot down the closest side wall (wallpaper shot) or hit cross-court to the opposite corner. The cross-court ceiling shot requires more power in the stroke because of the diagonal court distance to be covered as well as the need for accurate placement. If the ball is not hit at a sharp angle, the rebound forward will be away from the side wall and will provide for easy stroking room. A similar problem exists with a ceiling shot hit down-the-line if it does not "hug" the wall. Thus, although the ceiling shot is one of the easiest defensive strokes to learn, unless time is taken to practice placement, the true advantage of the shot cannot be achieved.

Points to Remember

1. When the ball hits the racquet, the angle of the racquet head must be directed to the spot on the front wall or ceiling that you want the ball to hit.

2. To hit a ceiling shot from a ball below waist level, open the racquet face.

3. Ceiling shots hit with an overhead stroke should contact the ball in front of the forward foot with an extended arm.

4. For the best advantage, angle ceiling shots so that they rebound into a back corner, preferably to your opponent's backhand.

5. Hitting a ceiling shot with too much force can result in the ball rebounding off the back wall and into play.

LOB SHOT

A **lob** shot is not played as often in competitive racquetball as other defensive shots. This is due to the popularity of the composite/graphite racquets and the use of pressurized balls. The **lob** is a shot that requires finesse and placement, not the power and strength for which this equipment was designed. Therefore, players that choose a fast-moving, power game often do not have the finesse necessary to hit a lob return.

A lob is struck with a technique similar to a ceiling shot hit from a ball falling below waist level. Both shots, whether hit with a forehand or backhand stroke, require an open racquet face. Contact with

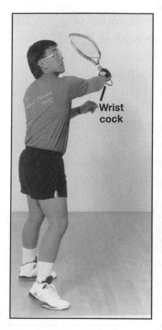

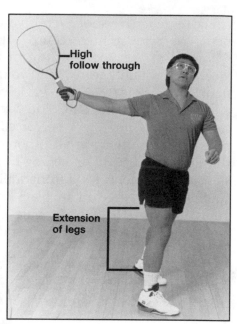

Wrist cock

Open racquet face

High follow through

Extension of legs

Backhand lob shot sequence.

the ball should be made inside the forward foot with an extended arm. Although not much force is required to hit this ball properly, the ball should be struck with your weight shifted toward the front wall. Finish the stroke with a follow-through high over your head. This arm motion and the racquet face angle serve to "lift" the ball.

Like the ceiling shot, the lob is returned high to the front wall, approximately 6 to 8 feet from the ceiling. However, the lob shot differs from the ceiling shot in that the ball never rebounds to touch the ceiling. Rather, the ball slowly moves along an arch close to the ceiling and high over center court, falling "dead" into a back corner with little or no rebound from the back wall. When perfectly hit, the slow movement of this ball allows you time to reposition yourself on the court, yet forces

your opponent into the disadvantage of a back-corner return.

Similar to the ceiling shot, a lob may be hit down-the-line (along the wall) or cross-court. If the lob is hit down-the-line, it is preferable to use a backhand shot towards the non-racquet side wall and a forehand shot to the racquet hand side wall for more control. A cross-court lob may be hit with either stroke. The purpose of both shots is to place the ball in a back-court position to prevent an offensive return. Thus, the lob presents many of the same problems to your opponent as the ceiling shot does. The reason why it is not hit more often is because it is a difficult shot to hit correctly. Since the ball does not rebound from the ceiling on the way to the back court, the ball, if hit too hard, will merely rebound off the back wall into a center court position. Thus, the

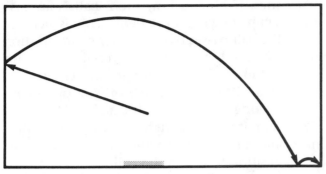

Proper lob defensive shot.

slow the ball and deaden its fall to the floor. For most beginners, the finesse with which this ball must be hit is hard to manage in a game situation where quick movements are necessary. Yet, the lob does offer an interesting variation for the player who can use it, including changing the pace of the game.

advantage of a back corner placement is lost. In addition, because the ball moves so slowly, it is easy to hit a strong return unless the lob is placed correctly. To minimize any possible rebound off the back wall, aim the lob so that the ball just brushes against a side wall close to the back corner. This "meeting" will

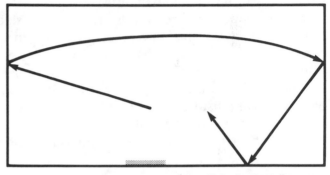

Lob shot rebounding into center court off the back wall.

Points to Remember

1. Remember to pivot the hips and hit the ball with an open racquet face.
2. Hit the ball as hard as you think necessary, then take some force off your swing.
3. Finish the stroke with a follow-through, with the racquet ending up high over your shoulder.
4. To take some power out of your shot, aim the ball to "brush" the side wall close to the back corner.
5. To be more effective, lob only to a back corner.

HIGH Z-BALL OR THREE-WALL SHOT

Like the other defensive shots, the **high Z or three-wall shot** is designed to move the opponent into a back corner. The high Z can be hit with either an overhead stroke from a high ball or a forehand or backhand stroke on a low ball return. To insure proper placement of the ball, the racquet head at contact must again be angled in the direction toward which the ball should travel. This means that the racquet face should be slightly open. In all other respects, the high Z stroke resembles one of the other defensive shots. The overhead stroke is similar to the overhead ceiling shot (see page 43) while the high Z, hit from low ball, is similar to the lob (see page 45).

As in other defensive shots, the high Z must be directed to hit high off the front wall. In addition, this shot must hit close to a front wall-side wall crotch (2-3 feet from it). As a result, the ball, after contact with the front wall, rebounds from the nearest side wall and moves diagonally across the court to the back corner. In essence, the movement of the ball describes a "Z" in the court. To follow this path, the ball must not hit the ceiling.

The placement of the ball on the front wall is critical to the effectiveness of this shot. If hit too low, the Z ball is an easy setup for your opponent. This is because the ball passes over a center court position when following the diagonal. A ball hit too low will pass through the center court area within arm's reach of your opponent. As long as the ball is hit high off the front wall, it will pass high over the center court and force your opponent into a back court position to return the ball.

Depending upon the strength of the hit, the Z ball may or may not hit a second side wall before touching the floor in the back corner. If hit hard, a second wall will be hit on the opposite side from the first before the ball rebounds to the floor. Thus, the name "three"-wall is often used to identify this shot. In this situation, the ball will "run the corner" by hitting the side wall, the back wall, and then the floor in succession.

Because the ball "covers" so much of the court on a Z-ball return, women and beginning level players often do not have a powerful enough stroke to hit the shot well. It is good to practice this shot often and feel confident about hitting it before trying a Z-ball return in a game situation.

Although a Z ball may be hit from anywhere in the court, you should try it from a center court position if your shot is weak. Stronger players will be effective with a high Z hit even from the back court. Because of the path followed by the ball, the Z is best hit to the opposite corner from your court position. Otherwise, the angle off the front wall will

High Z "three wall" defensive shot.

High Z defensive shot hitting floor before back corner.

not be great enough to cause a rebound along the diagonal.

The Z-ball or three-wall shot is very effective in causing a weak return, especially if the ball "runs the corner." In the back corner, there is little room to place a racquet and stroke through the ball unless timing is perfect and a good wrist snap is used. Therefore, this shot is often hit by more experienced players not only to force a bad court position but to "handcuff" the opponent as well.

Points to Remember

1. Hit the ball high off the front wall and close to the side wall-front wall crotch.

2. Use a stroke similar to an overhead ceiling shot for a ball over your shoulder and a lob return for waist-high balls.

3. Hit the ball hard enough to "run the corner" of the back court.

4. Hit the high Z to the corner opposite from the side of the court in which you are positioned.

AROUND-THE-WALL BALL

The around-the-wall ball is a defensive shot that hits three walls before touching the floor. It differs from the high Z shot in that the ball is first hit high to a side wall. The ball then rebounds to the front wall and finally to the opposite side wall from the initial hit. The closer to the front wall-side wall crotch the ball is aimed, the farther back on the opposite side wall the

ball will rebound. Since the purpose of this shot, like other defensive shots, is to force the opponent into a back court position, hitting close to a front corner is advised. If the ball strikes the first side wall too far from the front, the rebound will merely follow a path back to a center court position.

The stroke used to hit an around-the-wall ball is the same as for the high Z. This shot must be practiced, however, to insure that the proper racquet angle is used to hit the ball close to the front corner. Although not used often, the around-the-wall shot is probably most effective against a beginning player who has difficulty determining the rebound angle of the ball or against any player to change the pace of the game.

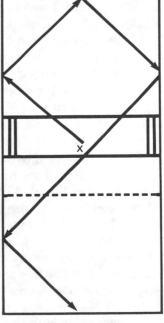

Around-the-wall ball.

Points to Remember

1. Hit the around-the-wall ball with the same technique used for a high Z ball.
2. Angle the ball close to the front wall-side wall crotch for the most effective hit.
3. Although not used often, this ball may be effective against beginning players and as a change-of-pace ball.

COMMON ERRORS AND HOW TO CORRECT THEM

1. My ceiling shots never hit the ceiling.
    A. If the ball is hit from a position below the waist, you are not hitting with an open racquet face to lift the ball high enough to hit the front wall and/or ceiling. If you are using an overhead stroke, the ball is probably too far in front of you when you contact it, or your racquet head is not angled toward the ceiling to direct the ball upward.
2. My ceiling shots hit the ceiling straight over my head.
    A. For both waist-level and overhead shots, you have angled your racquet too much, and the racquet face is almost parallel to the ceiling. In addition, with the overhead stroke, the ball is probably contacted over your head rather than off of your forward foot.
3. My ceiling shots rebound off the back wall into the playing area.
    A. You are hitting the ball too hard or with too little angle off the front wall. Aim closer to the front wall-ceiling crotch, and ease the force of your stroke.
4. My lob always hits the ceiling.
    A. You have too much force in your hit and/or too much angle on the racquet head. Hit the ball softer, and aim for a point lower on the front wall.
5. My lob always hits the back wall and rebounds to center court.
    A. Try to angle the hit more into the back corner of the court, then limit the force with which the ball is hit. If the ball does rebound into the court, it will at least be along the wall and will still provide little stroking room.
6. My high Z does not hit the back wall corner but goes straight into the back wall.
    A. Angle your hit into the front wall closer to the front wall-side wall crotch by changing the direction of the racquet head.
7. My high Z bounces too high off the back wall and gives my opponent an easy return.
    A. Hit the ball lower to the front wall, or softer and with more of an open racquet face so that the ball arches into the back court.
8. My high Z ball always rebounds off the front wall-side wall and bounces at center court, where it is returned by my opponent.
    A. Make sure that you are pivoting your hips before you stroke and that you are stepping into the ball. If you rely only on the strength of your arm to hit the ball, the force may not be great enough and the ball may not complete the diagonal of the court before touching the court floor.

CHAPTER 5

Serves in Racquetball

Serving is the most important offensive weapon in the arsenal of a beginning player. The serve can either "set" up a winning shot or prevent the opponent from scoring on the return of serve. The effectiveness of the serve is due to the controlled way in which it can be hit. This is the only time when you can contact the ball in a position of your choosing. Thus, you can play to your strengths and/or your opponent's weaknesses if you can consistently serve your best shot.

There are only five basic serves. Each serve, however, can be changed to give a slightly different look by varying the power with which it is hit, its height of rebound off the front wall, and/or the angle of rebound into the back court. With these variations, the basic serves can become hundreds of different shots. The wise player mixes these variations to keep the opponent guessing as to "where" the next ball will be served. However, the serve chosen should only be hit after thought is given to an opponent's

strengths and skills. Even a well-placed serve, if hit so that an opponent can return it with a favorite shot, is nothing more than a nice "setup." Similarly, a good player never hits a weak serve merely

Serving position on the court.

for the sake of variety if it is not obvious that an equally weak return will follow.

In order to make these serve variations effective, however, your serve must not become predictable, either from the position that you take in the service zone or from the technique with which you strike the ball. Ideally, all serves should be hit from a similar position on the court, with a similar stroke. Usually the center of the service zone and a normal forehand stroke are used. In this way, it is difficult, if not impossible, for your opponent to anticipate the direction of your serve. This means that variation in your serve must be a result of the amount of wrist snap or the position of the racquet face at the moment of contact with the ball. Either factor will affect the angle of hit or the power of the stroke.

Since you as the server are the only one who knows where the serve will be hit, you should also anticipate the placement of the returned ball. So take the time before each serve to not only plan the best serve, but the most likely return and how best to play the ball. Ideally, if the serve is not an outright winner, at least a poor return should occur, setting you up for your best offensive stroke.

For an opponent who you have never seen play, a good strategy is simply to serve to the backhand court with your best serve. If a player has a weakness, it is usually on the backhand side. This strategy should increase the odds of your winning the point with your serve.

The serve provides the server with the offensive advantage in the game. To serve without purpose or thought to your opponent's skill gives up this advantage and possibly the serve with it.

LEGAL SERVES

For a serve to be **legal**, the ball must be hit after it rebounds off the floor within the service zone. After contact with the racquet, the ball must strike the front wall before any other part of the court. However, the rebounding ball from the front wall may touch one side wall before falling to the floor behind the short line. The ball may not touch the floor in front of the short line or on the short line (short), a second side wall (two-wall), the ceiling (ceiling), or back wall (long) before the ball makes contact with the floor. A two-wall, short, long, or ceiling serve is an illegal serve (fault) and should not be played.

Most serves are hit with a forehand stroke. The server stands as far back as possible in the service zone with his/her hips pivoted to the side wall. Ideally, both feet should be placed along the short line. This provides as much service zone as possible

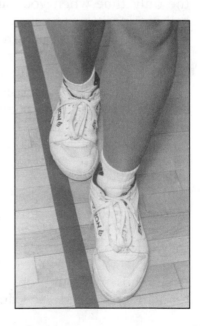

Foot placement to begin serve.

in which to step forward when contacting the ball. Stepping out of the service zone during the serve is illegal (fault).

To begin the serve, the ball falls off the fingertips of the non-racquet hand and is dropped to the floor. The hand should be extended to the front wall so that the ball is dropped as far forward in the service zone as possible. If the ball is not dropped close to the service line (front part of the service zone), the server will move past the ball when stepping forward to hit it. Thus, contact with the ball will occur off the back foot, and much of the force of the stroke will be lost.

Ball drop for service.

At the beginning of the serve, the racquet has already completed the backswing and is held perpendicular to the back wall. When the ball leaves the hand, the forward swing of the racquet begins. The angle of the racquet head and the height of the ball off the floor at contact are dependent upon the type of serve being hit. In any serve, however, it is essential to step into the stroke. The shifting of the body's weight from the back of the service zone to the foot that steps toward the service line provides additional power.

The serve, as any other stroke, is completed with a follow-through, the final position of the racquet being dependent upon the type of serve used. It is important to always hit "through" the ball rather than merely "punch" at it if a strong serve is desired. Although most serves are hit with a forehand stroke, on occasion a backhand or overhead stroke may be used.

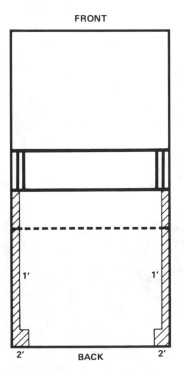

Court areas for served ball to be directed.

The following five serves are designed to follow the rules of service as well as place the opponent in a poor court position from which to hit an offensive return. As described with defensive strokes, this means hitting a ball into a back corner of the court. On all serves, it is important to keep the ball in the back corners and away from the midline of the court. A return from the middle of the court provides too many opportunities for offensive shots and prevents the server from holding a center court position. Thus, the following serves should be directed wide of the midline of the court and should only rebound back to a center court position after bouncing twice on the floor and being ruled a dead ball!

Lob

The **lob serve** is hit identically to the lob defensive shot, with the ball following the same path through the court (see page 45). The serve may be hit cross-court or down-the-line. As in the defensive lob, the ball must be hit high to the front wall, and the rebound should arch its way high over center court to die in a back court corner. To do this, the forward swing of the stroke must involve the racquet face

Backhand lob serve sequence.

held slightly open to the ceiling. The ball is hit below waist level and hit high off the front wall. The stroke is finished with the racquet held high over the forward shoulder. As in the defensive lob, a lob serve requires finesse rather than power.

To insure that the ball will die in the back court, the lob serve can graze a side wall close to the back wall. This rebound will slow the movement of the ball. As a result, the serve must be accurately directed to a corner. Accuracy in placement is critical. If the ball does not "handcuff" your opponent in the back corner, this slow-moving ball will be an easy setup for an offensive return. If this is difficult for you to do, hit the serve to the opponent's backhand. This will provide for a margin of error in placement because it will force a weak-side return.

To increase the accuracy of the lob serve to the backhand side of the court, many players will change their center court serving position and move to that side of the service zone. In addition, they will hit the ball with a backhand stroke using an open racquet face as on the forehand side. Although there is little deception in this maneuver, the difficulty in returning a lob serve comes not in surprising the opponent as much as in placing the ball. This court position allows for better placement because the ball is not hit at an angle. Rather, the racquet is parallel to the front wall and the ball is hit straight.

The lob is a good serve to use to change the pace of the game and to slow down a fast-moving opponent who likes to return serves hard to the front wall. The lob can be varied by hitting the serve at a "half lob" position, i.e., one which is about

shoulder height at the peak of its arch. Again, accuracy of placement is critical in the success of this serve.

Drive Serve

A **drive serve** is hit with a strong forehand stroke in order to insure good speed on the ball. To maximize the power in the stroke, it is essential that you begin the serve with your hips sideways to the front wall and that you meet the ball by stepping toward it during the forward swing. The ball should be contacted close to the ground — somewhere between the bent knee and the ankle. The forward swing should be level to the ground and the ball met just inside the forward foot. The follow-through should be low to the ground and should pull the shoulders around to finish the stroke facing the front wall. This serve resembles the kill shot in technique.

To be most effective, the drive serve must be hit low to the front wall to insure a low ball rebounding into the back court. Keeping the ball low adds to the difficulty in the return.

There is not one particular area of the court to which the drive serve should be directed. As in other serves, however, the serve should not rebound close to the midline of the back court. The ball can hit the side wall just past the short line (short corner drive serve), go straight into the back corner of the court, or hit the side wall several feet from the back wall and rebound "around the back corner." Any of these serves will be effective as long as you vary the angle of rebound off the front wall from serve to serve and keep the ball low. To do this, the angle of the racquet

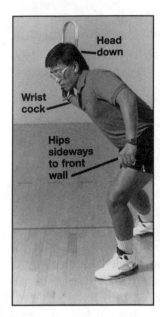
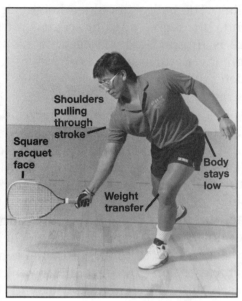

Head down

Wrist cock

Hips sideways to front wall

Shoulders pulling through stroke

Square racquet face

Weight transfer

Body stays low

Shoulders pulled through stroke

Follow through across body

Weight forward

Drive serve sequence.

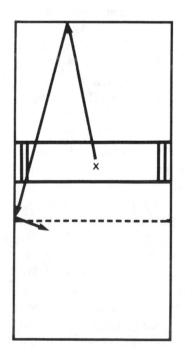
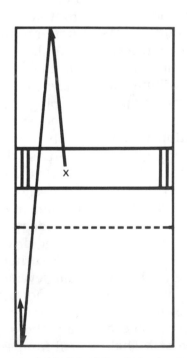
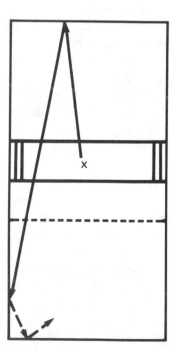

Variations of drive serves: behind short line, to back corner and off side wall.

face at ball contact must change with each hit. To prevent your opponent from anticipating the position of your serve, learn to hit a drive serve to the forehand and backhand sides of the court with equal skill. However, the backhand side is most effective in preventing offensive returns.

Z Serve

The **Z serve** can be divided into two distinct serves — a **high Z serve** and a **low Z serve**. The **high Z serve** is similar to the defensive Z shot in its movement around the court. This serve hits high on the front wall close to the front wall-side wall crotch. The ball rebounds to the nearest side wall, then travels high across the diagonal of the court to the opposite back corner. For the serve to be legal, however, the ball must hit the floor before touching another wall (unlike the defensive Z shot) and rebounding again. Thus, the movement of the ball on the court resembles the letter "Z".

This Z serve is hit with the same technique as the defensive Z shot (see page 47). The hips are turned to the side wall, racquet face is open, and contact with the ball is made inside the forward foot. However, the stroke cannot be as strong as the defensive shot because the ball must touch the floor before the opposite side wall is struck. Thus, like the lob serve, the high Z serve needs proper placement and finesse, rather than power, to be effective.

On the opposite extreme, the low Z ball requires power to make the shot work. The

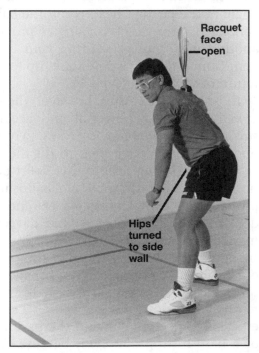

High Z serve.

low Z serve follows the same "Z" path around the court, but instead of traveling above shoulder height, the ball moves through the court close to the ground. Thus, this serve is hit low to the front wall, similar to the drive serve but with more strength because of the distance across the court that the ball must travel before touching the floor (i.e., past the short line).

The technique used to hit a **low Z serve** is similar to that for a kill shot (see page 27). The ball must be contacted inside the forward foot as the weight is shifted forward. The racquet should have a level swing at contact with the ball, and the arm movement must be completed with a follow-through. "Punching" at the ball by stopping the racquet's motion after hitting

the ball will only limit the power of the swing. A good wrist snap is also essential in providing the power necessary to hit a low Z ball.

The low Z may rebound to the floor anywhere along the side wall past the short line. If the ball is hit hard and close to the front wall-side wall crotch, the ball will rebound to the floor just behind the short line and hit the side wall. The extreme spin on the ball, due to the power of the stroke, will cause the ball to rebound almost straight off the side wall. Thus, an opponent positioned to hit a ball served deep into a back corner will be out of place to return this serve.

If the ball is hit several feet from the front wall-side wall crotch, the ball will be directed toward the back corner of the court. The different angles that can be used to hit the low Z serve depend on the angle of the racquet head when the ball is contacted. The variety of angles provides another means of preventing your opponent from knowing where to set up for the return of serve.

To be most successful, however, the low Z ball requires a powerful and accurate stroke. If the ball is moving too slowly, the opponent may be tempted to hit the ball as it passes through the center court position. For this reason, the low Z ball is used primarily by experienced players and seldom by beginning players who have not mastered shifting their body weight and snapping the wrist to increase the power of the serve. Beginning players usually rely on the high Z serve. Although this serve results in a slow-moving ball, it can be especially effective if hit to the backhand of a hard-hitting opponent because of its placement into a back corner.

Low Z serve.

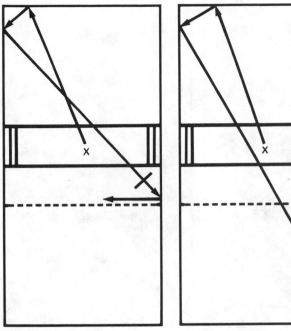

Low Z serve hitting past short line.

Low Z serve directed to the back corner of the court.

Overhead Serve

The **overhead serve** is rarely used in competitive racquetball, but it is a legal serve. It is hit with a stroke similar to that used in an overhead kill (see page 33), but the ball is not directed as low to the front wall as in the kill shot. The most difficult part of the stroke is starting the ball in play, since the ball must be hit only after rebounding off the floor. Therefore, to be contacted at a point over your head, the ball must hit the floor of the service zone with enough force so that it rebounds above your head and outstretched arm. Thus, the ball must be "thrown" to the floor rather than dropped. Because this throw must be done with your non-

racquet, i.e., non-dominant hand, the throw is a difficult one to make. If the ball is not thrown straight down, it will rebound out of the service area rather than overhead and cannot be hit. If the ball is not thrown with enough force, it will not bounce high enough for a proper overhead stroke. Therefore, if you anticipate using an overhead serve in a game, the throw should be practiced until its placement is consistent. If the throw is done correctly, the overhead stroke should contact the ball just inside the forward foot with the racquet held in an extended arm.

To hit the ball with the most control, the server should use a Western grip. The backswing and forward swing of the stroke resembles a circle, much like a tennis serve. The ball should be contacted at a point overhead after you have stepped onto your forward foot and shifted your body weight forward onto the ball of this foot. Until the point of impact, the racquet face should trail the wrist. Upon contact with the ball, the wrist and racquet should be snapped forward to direct the ball toward the bottom third of the front wall. This "snapping" will not only direct the ball downward, but increase the force of the stroke. The overhead serve is completed with a follow-through that brings the racquet downward across the body.

The ball should hit the front wall 5 to 6 feet off the floor. This will insure a low rebound into the back court. If the serve is hit lower, the ball will hit the floor in

Overhead serve sequence.

front of the short line and be called a fault. To rebound into a back corner, the ball must contact the front wall at least 1 foot on either side of the center when you are serving from the middle of the service zone. The overhead serve offers no unique advantage except a "different" look. Some beginning players like to hit an overhead serve because of its similarity to a tennis serve, with which they are familiar and can hit with power. However, the most difficult serves to return are not necessarily the most powerful, but rather those that are most accurately placed and rebound low into a back corner position. Because

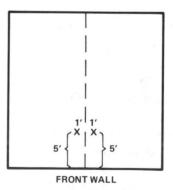

Target area on the front wall for an overhead serve

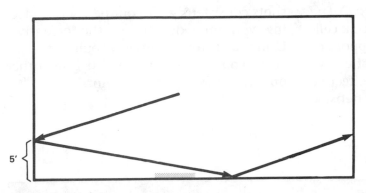

Rebound of an overhead serve off the front wall.

5′

the ball is hit down to the front wall with an overhead serve, the ball will often rebound off the floor with a high bounce. Thus, the ball may not be close to the floor in the back court. Therefore, keeping the ball low to the floor on the serve as done with the drive or low Z is more effective. This is why these serves are preferred by experienced players.

Garbage Serve

A **garbage serve** is hit with a forehand stroke. This serve "looks" much like a drive serve. The forward swing is level to the floor, and the ball is contacted inside the front foot. The force of the hit is dependent upon the speed of the swing and the snap of the wrist when the ball is contacted. The ball should not be hit as hard as it is in a drive serve, nor as softly as a lob. Yet, the follow-through should draw the racquet across the body to hit "through the ball." Although the ball should rebound wide of the midline of the court, it is not hit low to the floor or high to the ceiling. Rather, the ball rebounds

into the back court at a height between the opponent's waist and shoulder level off the floor. To hit the ball to this height, the server must contact the ball at a point higher off the floor than for a drive serve or with the racquet face slightly open. In general, the movement of the ball on the court gives the impression that the ball has been mis-hit.

This serve may or may not be hit with enough angle to rebound off a side wall before entering the back court. If it is, the ball should just brush the back wall so that the ball does not rebound back into play. In this respect, a garbage serve is similar to a half-lob.

If the serve is directed straight into the back corner, the ball must not be hit hard enough to rebound strongly off the back wall. A strong rebound at this point will

Garbage serve to back corner.

negate the value of the garbage serve. The strategy behind this serve is to force a ceiling return and/or prevent your opponent from hitting a kill shot or other offensive return. This strategy is especially effective with an opponent who can hit offensive shots consistently off your best serve, placing you immediately on the defensive. Using a garbage serve should at least "get" you past the serve and onto other opportunities to win the point.

Points to Remember

1. Unless a serve requires a different court position, serve from the center of the service zone with a forehand stroke so that you don't "signal" the type of serve you will hit.

2. Never serve the ball down the midline of the court, where an offensive return is easy to hit.

3. In addition to hitting the serve wide of the middle of the court, hit the ball low unless a garbage serve, lob, or high Z is desired.

4. Serve to the backhand side of the court if you don't know your opponent.

5. Practice serving to the right-hand side of the court in case you play a left-handed player (this will be the backhand side) and to provide variation in your serve.

6. Practice hitting your serves to rebound at different angles off the front wall, using varying heights off the floor and changing the power in your stroke.

7. The closer to the center of the front wall the ball is hit, the farther back in the court the ball will strike a side wall. The closer to a front wall corner the ball strikes, the closer to the front wall the ball will hit the side wall.

8. Use a lob or high Z ball to change the pace of the game and/or force a ceiling ball return.

COMMON ERRORS AND HOW TO CORRECT THEM

1. My lob serve hits the ceiling or the back wall.

   A. You are hitting the ball too hard or with too much angle toward the ceiling. Hit the ball softer and with less angle, i.e., so that the ball hits lower on the front wall.

2. My drive serve rebounds off the back wall into the center court.

   A. Drop you knees closer to the ground so that you can drop your racquet lower to the floor. This will allow you to contact the ball when it is closer to the floor. Hitting a lower ball into the back court will lessen the chance of a rebound off the back wall. In addition, angling the ball to hit a side wall before it touches the back court floor should "deaden" the movement of the ball into the back court and prevent a hard rebound from the back wall.

3. My Z ball hits two side walls before it hits the floor.

   A. Hit the ball farther from the front corner and closer to the center of the front wall so that the ball will rebound to a point farther into the back court. Another correction would be to hit the ball with less stroking power while keeping the same forward swing to maintain the height of the ball's contact with the front wall.

4. My drive serve "pops" off the front wall and rebounds high into the back court.

   A. You probably are standing up as you make contact with the ball during the serve. If you do not maintain a low position to the floor throughout the forward swing, the ball will be lifted along with your body and rebound up off the front wall. Make sure that you have followed through your serving motion before you come to a ready position to prepare for the return of serve.

5. My garbage serve hits straight into the back wall.

   A. You are hitting the serve too hard. Take some power off your stroke, and angle the racquet head slightly toward the ceiling upon contact with the ball.

6. My serves go straight down the center of the court.

   A. You are not hitting the ball with enough angle (toward a front wall corner). This can be corrected in one of two ways: (1) Throw the ball out in front of you and toward your backhand side if you want to hit the ball to the side wall behind you. Throw the ball slightly behind the front foot and toward your forehand side if you want to hit the ball toward the side wall that you are facing. (2) Always throw the ball in the same place relative to your body, but concentrate on breaking you wrist upon contact with the ball if you want to serve to the side wall behind you. Open up your wrist (laid back position) if you want to hit toward the side wall that you are facing.

   Continued

This technique is the best because it will disguise your service direction until contact is made.

7. My overhead serve always hits the floor in front of the short line.

   A.   You are hitting the ball too low to the front wall. Check to see if you are hitting the ball just inside your forward foot and if your racquet head is angled in the direction in which you want the ball to go. If so, then you must aim at a higher point off the floor for the ball to contact the front wall. To do this, don't snap your wrist as much when contacting the ball, and/or hit the ball when it is at a higher point on its rebound.

CHAPTER 6

Use of Back Wall and Corners

Offensive and defensive strokes comprise the primary skills involved in the game of racquetball, but there is also skill needed to play the court correctly. Using the walls to your advantage requires both thought and practice.

THE BACK WALL

Up to now, this book has ignored the part of racquetball that makes it an interesting and challenging game — the use of the **back wall**. Beginning players often "learn to play" racquetball by avoiding the back wall completely. As a result, they are not really playing four-wall racquetball. This type of play puts these players at a disadvantage when facing an opponent who uses the whole court. Without using the back wall as a playable surface, two problems occur: (1) any ball that gets past your position in the court is "out of play" with no chance for you to retrieve it and (2) in order to prevent balls from getting past you, players use unorthodox strokes with unpredictable results to return the ball. Thus, when not using the back wall, players must often resort to merely hitting the ball to keep it in play rather than directing it. This is a strategy we refer to as "Battleball."

When playing "Battleball," the player maintains a center court position and hits every ball within reach as hard as possible back to the middle of the front wall — the strategy being, if the ball is hit hard to the front wall, it may rebound past the opponent and score a point. Of course, this tactic may work against another "Battleball" player, but the experienced opponent will skillfully use the back wall to keep the ball in play. Only until you feel confident enough to use the back wall will you be able to play more than "Battleball" on the racquetball court.

HAVE PATIENCE...

The key factor in using the back wall well is PATIENCE — having the patience to let a ball intentionally go past you. Before you can play with "patience," you must develop confidence in your ability to play balls on the rebound off the back wall. Part of this confidence comes from many hours of court practice and another part from an understanding of why the back wall is helpful.

BACK WALL ADVANTAGE

The use of the back wall is important because it provides several **advantages** during the game. First, a ball that goes past you into the back court can still be hit as it rebounds off the back wall. Second, by waiting for balls to rebound off the back wall, you can move into a better position for hitting a forehand or backhand stroke, i.e., setup for the return. If the ball is hit before the back wall rebound, often it is above or below the ideal hitting area. It is impossible to practice hitting balls at all positions relative to your body. Thus, always adjusting your court position so that the ball is at the same place relative to your forehand or backhand stroke will insure a consistent hit. This means that you will be in control of the ball's movement around the court and consequently your opponent's court position as well. Finally, waiting for the rebound affords you more time to "see" where your opponent is waiting in the court and to plan the most effective offensive return. Thus, the use of the back wall adds to your ability to control the movement of the ball, your opponent's court position and to potentially gain an offensive advantage.

GETTING IN POSITION

In order to **position** yourself to hit a good return off the back wall, you must

never lose eye contact with the ball or turn your back to the front wall. The most critical mistake that players make when returning balls off the back wall is turning to face the back wall when stroking the ball. As a result, a normal forehand or backhand stroke cannot be used because the ball would be hit into the side wall. Thus, out of desperation, the player facing the back wall resorts to flipping the ball over the shoulder, hitting a blind shot toward the front. This shot does not allow you to control and direct the movement of the ball — only to keep it in play. Thus, the only way to successfully use the back wall is to pivot your hips for a forehand or backhand return and adjust your position relative to the ball's rebound by cross-stepping up or back. The critical decision

Moving for a back wall return.

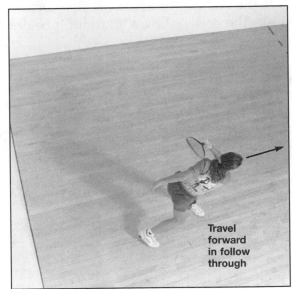

Watching the ball as it rebounds to back wall.

to be made when returning a ball from the back wall is whether to use a forehand or backhand shot. This decision must be made quickly, and the pivot to the appropriate side should follow immediately. It is easy to judge the side from which most balls should be hit. However, balls that follow the diagonal of the court are more difficult to play. Usually these balls begin in the front court and end in the back court at the opposite corner. Therefore, a ball that begins on your left side becomes a hit from the right side, and you must pivot to the opposite corner from where the ball rebounds in the front court. Practicing for these balls on the court is the best way to learn how to position yourself.

To hit any ball off the back wall properly, a player can never afford to stop watching the ball as it rebounds off the front wall for the back wall hit. Follow the ball from your pivot position, moving only your eyes to keep the ball in sight.

Once the pivot to the appropriate side has been made, proper positioning for the rebound will either allow you to "make or miss" the shot. It is hard to learn how to adjust your position for the ball without going into the court and practicing. But a few general guidelines may be helpful in getting you started.

If the ball has touched the floor before it hits the back wall, you must hit it before it touches the floor again, i.e., directly off the rebound. Because it has touched the floor, the ball's bounce is deadened and will not rebound far off the back wall. Thus, you will need to move close to the back wall to hit the ball. However, if the ball hits the back wall without touching the floor, you should wait for the ball to hit the floor before making contact with it. But be prepared to move forward in the court, because the ball will rebound sharply off the wall and "run" toward the front court area. In either case, you need to position yourself so that at the point of contact, the ball will be hit inside the forward foot with the proper forehand or backhand stroking motion.

A more difficult shot to return is the back wall rebound of a lob or ceiling shot

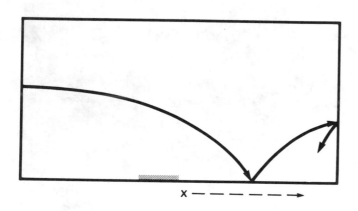

Rebound of ball off the back wall after hitting the court floor.

Rebound of the ball off the back wall, running into a center court position

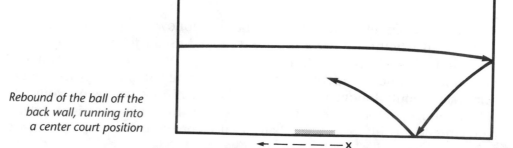

Backhand return off back wall.

that just grazes the back wall, dies, and falls to the floor. With either shot, the ball has already touched the floor. Therefore, the ball must be hit immediately after contact with the back wall. The only way to successfully hit this type of rebound is with a sharp wrist snap on the racquet. Station the racquet between the path of the ball and the wall. As the ball passes the face of the racquet, flip the racquet forward with a sharp wrist motion. The best return on this ball is a defensive shot directed toward the top of the front wall. This way if the shot is weak, the ball will still make contact somewhere on the front wall surface. In addition, a defensive return will give you time to reposition yourself on the court.

Back wall shot off a ball grazing back wall.

If during a game, you are not able to return the ball off the back wall, you may have to hit the ball as it is falling toward you, before it strikes the back wall. In this case, the best shot to use is an overhead ceiling shot (see page 43). With this return, you will keep the ball in play and have an opportunity to later win the rally.

Never jump to hit these balls. All balls will eventually fall to within arm's reach. If the ball hits so high off the back wall that it can't be hit with an outstretched arm, wait for the rebound. Jumping only adds another factor to control when trying to hit the ball perfectly. Jumping for the ball is a sign of IMPATIENCE.

Points to Remember

1. To hit a ball off the back wall, pivot 90 degrees to the side from which the shot is to be taken, and cross-step forward or backward to a court position where the ball will rebound.

2. Watch the ball at all times.

3. If the ball touches the floor before the back wall, the rebound will drop close the back wall.

4. If the ball hits the back wall before touching the floor, the ball will rebound into a mid to center court position.

5. Balls that rebound strongly off the back wall can be returned with a defensive or offensive shot using either a backhand or forehand stroke.

6. Hitting a ball that grazes the back wall should be returned by emphasizing the wrist snap and placing the racquet along the wall, hitting a defensive return as the ball falls past the face of the racquet.

HITTING INTO THE BACK WALL

Rather than properly using the **back wall**, a temptation for a beginning player is to hit the ball into the back wall with the hope that it will rebound the length of the court to the front wall. This type of hit is more likely to occur if the player turns completely around to face the back wall when playing the rebound. For some players, hitting into the back wall becomes a favorite shot. Unfortunately, the more this shot is relied on, the weaker your game

will be. First, it is impossible to hit an offensive shot off an "into-the-back-wall" hit. Second, even defensive shots are unreliable from this return because you are facing away from the front wall, making it almost impossible to "aim" the ball. Finally, with the distance the ball must travel (more than the full length of the court), the ball becomes a slow-moving, easy target for your opponent to return. Thus, hitting the ball into the back wall

Hitting into the back wall.

served ball that you cannot place your racquet between it and the wall to stroke it forward.

USING THE BACK WALL

If a back wall return must be used, be sure to contact the ball with an upward scooping motion to angle the rebound above your head and high toward the front wall. The ball must be hit hard.

Never hit the ball into the back wall from a mid or center court position. Not only is this bad strategy, but your opponent may be in the back court and consequently, in the path of the ball. Standing 10-15 feet away from a hit ball gives your opponent very little time to duck. Many serious injuries have resulted from this type of play.

The player who wants to win at racquetball cannot afford to rely on such an ineffective and dangerous shot. To avoid placing yourself in the position of hitting the ball into the back wall, remember (1) never turn 180 degrees to face the back wall to return a ball and (2) move quickly to meet the ball in the court rather than being caught out of position with no other shot available.

should only be used as a "last resort shot," when there is no other way of keeping the ball in play.

The only two occasions where this situation is likely to occur (short of your moving lazily to a good court position) is (1) off a passing shot that beats you into the back court and (2) a ball that falls so close to the back wall from a ceiling, lob, or

Points to Remember

1. Hitting into the back wall is a desperation shot and provides little advantage to the player except to keep the ball in play.

2. Hitting into the back wall should never be done from a center or mid court position.

3. When returning the ball to the back wall, use a scooping stroke to lift the ball over your head and past your face.

4. Hit the ball hard, it must travel more than the length of the court.

CORNER SHOTS

Another important return to learn is hitting a ball that rebounds to a back **corner.** For most players, this is the most difficult shot in the game. To contact a corner ball, you must contend with the back and side walls simultaneously. Without any room to stroke the ball, an effective offensive shot is eliminated, and you can only hope for a good defensive return.

It is important with a corner shot to pivot immediately toward the corner in which the ball will rebound while keeping

Hitting out of the corner.

the ball in view. The success of this return is dependent upon your ability to position yourself properly in relation to the ball's movement. Anticipate the ball's rebound, and maintain a court position behind the forward bounce. From this position you can still step into the ball to make contact. If the ball does not rebound with enough force to allow you to hit the ball with a forward swing, then the power in the hit must come from the wrist snap.

The key to a successful corner shot return is having the patience to wait for the ball to rebound off the back wall. Most beginners do not have the patience to wait and swing wildly as the ball comes within reach. Another mistake commonly made is using a wide, sweeping swing with an extended arm, using the shoulder to supply the force behind the stroke. Not only is this "big" arm swing dangerous, but there is no room for this type of "tennis" stroke in the corner of the court.

Contact with a corner hit that has little rebound off the back wall should be made with an open racquet face. This will direct the ball toward the ceiling and give you more margin for error. If the ball rebounds away from the back wall, any forehand or backhand return can be used. Most players, however, choose a defensive return because of their back court position. Therefore, the return of a corner ball should be considered successful if a good defensive shot is hit.

Points to Remember

1. For all corner shots, position yourself behind the rebound so that you can step into the ball to return it.

2. Avoid using a big arm swing, especially if the ball is rebounding tightly into the corner; instead, rely on a wrist snap.

3. If the ball does not rebound strongly out of the corner, hit a defensive ceiling shot rather than trying for an offensive return.

4. A ball that rebounds hard off the corner may be returned with any type of shot.

COMMON ERRORS AND HOW TO CORRECT THEM

1. When I try to return a ball from a back corner, my racquet always hits a side wall.

   A. You are using a large arm swing to hit the ball rather than relying on the wrist snap. Place the racquet along the anticipated path of the ball, and contact the ball when it moves past the racquet face using a sharp wrist snap.

2. When I hit a rebound off the back wall, my return always hits a side wall.

   A. Check to see if you are turning your hips to face the back wall rather than only making a pivot toward the side wall. This body position will cause you to hit the ball into a side wall rather than forward.

   B. When hitting the ball, the racquet face may also be directed at a side wall if you are contacting the ball either off your back foot or too far in front of your forward foot. Try repositioning yourself when hitting a back wall shot so that contact is made with the ball in proper position relative to your body for the stroke you are using.

CHAPTER 7

Putting the Strokes Together: Non-Thinking Strategy

As a beginning player on the court, your **strategy** is limited by your skill level. As you become more proficient with a variety of shots and feel confident enough to use them in a game situation, your **strategy** will change accordingly. However, with limited playing skills, success on the court is most easily obtained using a defensive strategy. This means that your objective during each rally is to keep the ball in play with defensive shots while maintaining a good court position. Points, therefore, are won with this strategy, not because you make an outstanding offensive shot, but because your opponent makes errors in his/her return. At the beginning level, unforced errors account for over half of the points scored. Therefore, if you can keep the ball in play with defensive shots, the odds are on your side that your opponent will lose the rally. This may not be as satisfying as hitting a winning shot, but it is more productive in the end. This is called the "non-thinking" strategy because few decisions are made during play. The only decision that you must make is WHICH defensive shot to hit.

Why are defensive shots a good choice for a beginning player? Simply because these shots are easiest to learn and consistently hit correctly. Defensive shots can be hit hard or soft from anywhere on the court, and there is more room for error in their placement while still being strategically effective. However, to successfully play a defensive game, several points should be remembered.

CONCENTRATE AND WATCH THE BALL

To follow any strategy when playing racquetball, you must **concentrate** on the game and **watch the ball**. Any mental distractions should be left outside the court to improve your concentration on the game for the players' safety and the fun of the game. A player who is distracted by other thoughts may end up at the painful end of a stroke, or at the very least missing easy-to-hit shots.

Concentrate and watch the ball.

Part of concentrating on the game requires that you watch the ball at all times. This is true regardless of whether it is your turn to hit the ball or not. The movement of the ball is so fast around the court with the potential to quickly change directions that losing eye contact with the ball usually results in an inability to properly "set up" for the stroke in time. Therefore, your return may result in loss of a point simply because of your poor court position.

SERVE YOUR BEST

Even though you are following a defensive strategy, you can and should use your serve to its offensive advantage. This means: **serve your best.** "Best" can be defined in two ways: (1) either the serve that you hit well with predictable results or (2) the serve that may not be skillfully

Moving and watching the ball.

hit but attacks the opponent's weakness in service return. How would you choose between these two options? Usually, the choice is automatic. If a particular type of serve (i.e., lob to the backhand side) always gains a point for you through a faulty return, then use it. If your opponent has no consistent weakness with one type of serve, then use your most skilled serve — one that is always properly placed and hit with authority.

Unfortunately, when playing a new opponent, it will take time and possibly some "lost serves" before you can discover a player's weakness or which serve is working best for you that day. In this case, a good strategy is to serve to the opponent's

Serve to the back corner.

backhand. For most beginning players, the backhand suffers from a lack of practice because forehand strokes are hit with more success. Therefore, backhand strokes are not as skillfully controlled.

In addition to hitting toward the backhand side, the effectiveness of any serve can be increased if the ball is hit so that the rebound lands close to a side wall in a back corner. This court position makes the serve more difficult to return with an offensive stroke. Another benefit of this serve placement is that your opponent must move from the middle of the court to return the ball. Consequently, this court position is open for you to occupy.

If you are still confused as to how to serve the ball, use your own experience as a guide. The serve that is most difficult for you to return will be the most difficult for your opponent as well, assuming that both of you are at similar skill levels. Remember — your service strategy does not suggest that a serve is only successful if it is an "ace." Rather, the serve is useful if a weak return follows (i.e., a ball that is neither an offensive nor a good defensive shot). This type of return sets you up for an easy offensive shot to the front wall and a point.

KEEPING A CENTER COURT POSITION

In a game involving beginning players, balls often pass through the **center court** after rebounding off the front wall. This is because the novice player returns most balls to the center of the front wall. Therefore, standing 1 to 3 feet behind the short line and an equal distance from either side wall will give you the best position to reach most balls. A center court position is suggested not only because more balls travel through this area than any other part of the court, but from here, the player can reach balls that rebound short or long or that run along either wall.

How do you gain and maintain this strategic center court position? If you are serving, the problem is easily solved. When playing singles, the server usually serves from a position close to the center of the service zone. This position is taken for two reasons. First, if all serves are hit from the same place in the service zone, there is little chance of the server's court position "giving away" the type of serve that is going to be hit. Second, this position allows easy access to the strategic playing position in center court. As soon

as the server is allowed to leave the service zone, this player should back up into the center court. Because of the server's proximity to center court, a few quick steps will do the job. Unfortunately, beginning players often choose to turn, face the back wall (and the receiver who is hitting the ball), and move to a center court position while "watching" the serve. Not only is this dangerous because it exposes the server to a direct "in-the-face" return off the receiver's racquet, but a quick return of serve may find the server's back to the front wall as the ball rebounds. Thus, backing up to center court while using peripheral vision to follow the ball is not only the safest, but the most effective tactic.

Maintaining this court position after the serve is merely a matter of keeping your opponent out of it. To do this, consistently place your shots so that the rebound off the front wall is wide of the middle of the court and deep into a back

Service position in service zone.

Center court position, safely watching the ball.

court position. A ceiling, lob, or high Z ball are all effective in placing the ball deep into a back court corner. To return these shots, your opponent must follow the ball to the back court, leaving the center court position open for you to occupy. As long as your returns are hit in this manner, the center court will always be open.

One precaution that beginners must be aware of is to avoid hitting the ball hard enough to allow it to rebound off the back wall and into the center court. Since the player hitting the ball cannot be impeded by the opponent, a rebound of this type would force you to move out of a center court position.

Similarly, if you are receiving the serve, hitting a defensive stroke (such as the ceiling, lob, or high Z) along a side wall into a back corner or even a cross-court return will open the center court as the server chases your return. Therefore, you should be ready to move to the center court position once your opponent has vacated this area. The usual movement on a racquetball court consists of a constant shifting of position in and out of the center court.

Thus the non-thinking strategy suggests returning to the center court position after each shot as quickly as possible, or maintaining this position until moving for a ball forces you out. At the same time,

Receiving serve

Hitting a cross court return

Move to center court

Moving the server out of a center court position.

continue to hit defensive shots away from the midline of court to keep your opponent out of this strategic court area.

MOVING TO THE BALL

The reason why you can move your opponent out of a center court position is simply because this player must leave center court to **play the ball.** Unfortunately, many beginning players are content to hit the ball if it is within an arm's reach regardless of where the ball is in relation to their body. This means using unorthodox strokes, few of which a player has practiced. Returns hit in this way will serve only to rebound the ball to the front wall rather than place it. This tactic keeps the ball in play but provides neither an offensive nor a defensive advantage. Since you have practiced hitting forehand and backhand shots, why not use them! The

Moving directly to the ball.

key to success in racquetball is not only knowing where to hit the ball to keep your opponent at a disadvantage, but being able to do it. Using tried and true strokes will produce better game results than a contrived, over-the-shoulder "punch."

To hit the ball with the same stroke requires that you move to a court position where the best contact with the ball can be made. Usually, this strategy involves playing balls off the back wall to allow the ball to drop from shoulder height as it moves through the court to a lower position off the back wall rebound. Low balls can be hit with the same forehand and backhand strokes by bending your knees and dropping your waist closer to the ground. The stroking technique remains the same.

Instead of waiting for the ball to drop from an overhead position to within arm's reach, however, many beginning players jump to reach the ball. Jumping is never advised as a means of getting to the ball for three reasons. First, all balls will eventually fall to the floor and could be hit from waist level. Second, jumping for the ball prevents you from stepping into the stroke and generating more power in the swing. Third, the jumping is another factor that must be controlled to hit a good return. Therefore, jumping is neither necessary nor practical as a means of moving to the ball. This is one situation where you must wait for the ball to come to you.

Finally, when adjusting your court position to move to the ball for the best hit, it is important to move where the ball will be rather than chasing the ball around the court. Always take the shortest and most direct path to the ball's rebound. If you

find this hard to do, spend some time in a court alone, hitting the ball at various angles into the front wall, and watch the ball's movement. For beginning players who have not played a court game before, the rebound angles and movement of the ball must be learned through experience.

PLAYING THE DEFENSIVE GAME

In summary, playing the **defensive game** does not mean that the beginning player should never hit an offensive shot. Rather, this strategy tries to simplify the game by minimizing the options available to the player. To some extent, these options are already minimized by the skill of the player and the type of shot available. If an offensive shot can be made successfully, by all means use it to end the rally. However, the beginning player usually must concentrate on merely "staying in the game" and "keeping the ball in play," especially with a more experienced opponent. The defensive game is designed to do this. In general, the defensive game relies only on your ability to hit a defensive shot and keep your opponent away from the offensive center court position. This means consistently hitting high lobs, high Z balls, or three-wall shots to a back corner while maintaining the center court position yourself. In this type of game you do not "win" the game so much as the opponent "loses" it. Regardless, you are still the victor. This is "non-thinking" strategy, because your return to the front wall is predetermined before the ball leaves your racquet — a defensive shot to the opponent's backhand corner.

The other part of the "non-thinking" strategy is your court position. Except for the time when you are moving to hit the ball, always station yourself in the offensive center court position. This means that as soon as the ball leaves your racquet and you can move without interfering with your opponent, return (if necessary) to the center court position. Too often, a beginning player hits the ball and remains stationary, waiting to see where the opponent will hit the ball. If you are positioned on one side of the court and/or in the front or back court, you are "giving away" part of the court. A ball hit to the opposite side, short or long, would be almost impossible to return. Therefore, hit the ball and MOVE. Where? To the center court.

This strategy is not only practical for the beginner, but for any player who is facing a stronger, quicker, and perhaps more skilled opponent. The defensive game takes away the opponent's offensive opportunities and slows the tempo of the game. If you are not able to move fast enough to position yourself for good returns, then hitting a defensive return will help to slow the ball's movement and provide more time to get in position for the next shot.

Women can find a defensive game especially effective against men. Usually men are stronger and faster and hit the ball with more power. Forcing the man to always return off slower-moving defensive shots will minimize this advantage. In addition, the defensive shot will give you some "breathing room" — time to reposition yourself in the center court and "catch your breath."

Points to Remember:

1. The defensive game is not designed for you to win points, but rather to prevent you from losing points.

2. Begin on the offensive with your best serve or at least with a serve that will prevent your opponent from hitting an offensive return.

3. After the serve, move to the center court position, and return to it after each hit.

4. Hit defensive shots on all your returns and preferably to the opponent's weak side (usually backhand).

5. Realize that defensive shots can also slow down the game and help to maintain the playing tempo at a speed at which you can successfully compete.

6. Use offensive shots only if they are "sure" winners; otherwise, you are "giving" away a point.

CHAPTER 8

Putting the Strokes Together: Thinking Strategy

The **"non-thinking" strategy** of the defensive game becomes ineffective as a player's skills improve. When a player is able to add offensive strokes to his/her game with a predictable outcome, a **"thinking strategy"** must be used. The strategy in this type of game not only involves keeping the opponent out of an offensive court position, but takes advantage of the opponent's weaknesses in skill or court position through ball placement and shot selection.

During this game, shots are varied but purposeful. This is a THINKING strategy that calls for the player to use a variety of defensive and offensive shots. Thus, points are won rather than lost, and the style of play is more aggressive. How successful a thinking/offensive strategy can be depends upon the skill level of the players.

HOW TO CHOOSE THE RIGHT SERVE

Minimally, the **"right"** serve is one in which an offensive shot is not returned.

Ideally, the **"right"** serve results in no return to the front wall or in such a weak return that the server can hit a winning shot immediately. Which serve will be most effective in achieving these goals will vary from opponent to opponent.

It is always a good strategy to begin by hitting your best serve to your opponent's backhand. Even if a backhand serve is anticipated, the skill of your serve should score a point. Relying continually on this serve, however, will only give your opponent an opportunity to practice returning it! Thus, variety in your serves will be the ultimate key to success at this level of play. How can you add variety to the serve? Changing the speed of the serve, the height to the front wall, the rebound angle to the back court, or the depth to which the ball is hit in the court will all give your serve a "new look." The same basic serve can be hit to either side, short or long, high or low, hard or slow. In general, low, hard-hit serves (like the drive, low Z) are more effective in "forcing" a

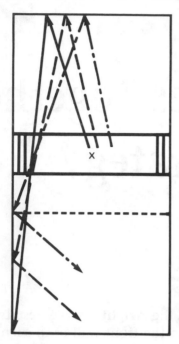

Changing the angle of the serve will cause a change in the depth of the rebound into the back court.

poor return; however, this type of serve is more difficult to control. High, softer serves such as the lob, high Z, and garbage serve are not as difficult to hit and, due to their placement, result in a ceiling shot return rather than an offensive shot.

Choosing the most effective serve for the game situation varies from service to service and depends on how well you are playing. If the strengths of your game outnumber the strengths of your opponent, you can play your hard serve (drive, low Z) knowing that your skill should win the point. If the opponent's strengths outnumber yours, then you need to play to a weakness and serve for a defensive return. Continue to keep your opponent on the defensive until an offensive opportunity

opens for you. Consequently, the type of serve that you choose will set the tone for your game strategy: attack and try to outgun your opponent or play a more conservative game that keeps the opponent off the offensive.

You may also serve effectively to your opponent's forehand. Many players practice serving only to the backhand side. Serving only to this side of the court will take away some of the variety in your serve and allow your opponent to anticipate where the ball will be directed.

A serve to the forehand side can be effective if it is properly hit and wide of center. If this is your opponent's strong stroke, then do not serve a hard-hit ball to the forehand court. Rather, use a lob or high Z serve to force a defensive return. If your opponent does not have a strong forehand shot, a low drive serve will usually force a down-the-line return on the same side of the court. If you anticipate this return and position yourself a step closer to the side wall, your second shot of the rally can be a winner. Therefore, a serve can also be effective if the return of that serve "sets" you up for an offensive shot regardless of how well the return of serve is hit.

Another rule of strategy suggests that when you are tired, hit your hardest serves. Assuming that you are not the player in worse shape, your feeling of fatigue will undoubtedly be matched by your opponent. The harder the serve, the faster it must be reacted to. A tired player reacts slower and/or returns the ball with less power than a fresh opponent. Take advantage of your ability to control the tempo of the game by serving hard and keeping up the pressure. This would be an excellent time to hit a short drive serve if your opponent is playing deep in the back court.

Remember — with the serve, you control the game. It is the only time during play when you determine where the ball will be when you hit it. Use this advantage to set the tempo of the game, emphasize your strong skills, and force your opponent to rely on his/her weaknesses. At the very least, if a point is not won with the serve, you must be sure that it is not LOST because of a weak serve.

ANTICIPATING YOUR OPPONENT'S SHOT

The beginning player is restricted to playing from a center court position during a rally due to his/her inability to *anticipate ball movement* and/or lack of

playing skill. Most shots can be easily hit from the center court, and most poorly placed balls generally rebound to this area. Therefore, it is an ideal location for the novice player. The experienced player, however, is usually facing an opponent whose shot selection is varied, and ball control allows more skill in court placement. Thus, rather than "playing the court," as the beginning player does, the more experienced player plays the shot. This means that you should anticipate the best return that your opponent can hit and begin moving for the ball's predicted path before it is hit.

Anticipating a shot is not always guesswork. Many players will "signal" the kind of shot that they are going to make merely by their body position relative to the ball. Since you are watching the ball at all times, you can simultaneously watch your

Short drive serve to the forehand side.

Racquetball angle indicating a ceiling or Z-ball return.

USING THE COURT WISELY

A player's **court position** can be used to an advantage in two ways. One is to "take away" the opponent's "best shot" — that shot which has a high probability of being a winner — and the second is to keep your opponent moving in the court with the purpose of tiring this player out.

The first use of the court requires that you maintain a court position to either (1) make your opponent's best return shot impossible to hit or (2) place you in the ideal position to hit the ball off this return. This tactic is only important when your opponent has been successful in scoring consistently off one return. To prevent losing more points to this shot, you must in essence "block" it. An example of blocking a shot would be staying to the left of center to "discourage" a down-the-line shot in order to force a weaker cross-court return. To be effective in "blocking" shots, however, your court position must be fixed before the opponent returns the ball — otherwise no blocking has occurred. Remember — the purpose of positioning yourself on the court in this manner is to eliminate this shot as one of your opponent's options.

The object of the second use of the court is to literally keep your opponent running. Shot selection is determined not only by the other player's weaknesses, but also with consideration as to how far your opponent would have to move to get to the ball. For example, if you have just hit the ball to the backhand side, return the ball to the forehand side. Varying placement of the ball short and long is also effective if your opponent has not

opponent set up to hit the ball. Notice changes in stance (hip and foot placement), racquet head angle (i.e., close to a back wall or in center court). Look for any body or racquet position that is consistent with one particular shot. If nothing is apparent but you are continually beaten by one particular return, use the game situation and court position as a guide as to when that shot would be used, then move to cover it.

To help anticipate the ball's movement, especially how hard the ball is hit, use your ears as well as your eyes. The sound of the ball hitting the racquet can give you a clue as to the power of the stroke. A strong hit will make a louder sound against the strings of the racquet than an easy return or mis-hit. Listen to the sound of the hit to anticipate how hard and fast the ball will rebound off the front wall.

Blocking a down-the-line return.

anticipated the short ball and set up for this return. Even the most conditioned player will fatigue after long rallies where the ball must be hit from all parts of the court. This tactic can be especially valuable at the end of the game when fatigue causes slower reaction and movement times.

"RETURNING" TO THE OFFENSIVE POSITION

Since the serve provides the server with the first opportunity to score, the server is considered to be the offensive player. As such, the server is initially in control of the game. Thus, it is the job of the receiver to regain the serve and thus the **offense**. The first step in this strategy requires that

you move the opponent out of the center court position. Any of the defensive strokes or a down-the-line or cross-court return will work equally as well. The preference for the latter two shots is that they are offensive returns and have the potential for ending the rally immediately. However, neither of these strokes should be hit unless the ball is served at knee level or below. Balls that are served high off the front wall or that rebound high into the back court (lob, Z ball, ceiling) should be hit with your best defensive return. With any of these returns, the server will be pulled out of the center court position, which you can now assume. Consequently, you have eliminated the server's offensive court advantage and regained this position yourself.

To make the best return off serves that rebound off the floor high against the back wall, make it a practice to hit the serves as soon after the floor bounce as possible. If you allow the ball to strike the back wall, you must hit the ball as it falls to the floor, possibly very close to the corner. Hitting the serve before it touches the back wall will usually give you a better shot opportunity. Similarly, balls that would "run the corner" should be taken before the corner is hit. Otherwise, you will face a very difficult return. This may mean positioning yourself a step or two closer to the front wall and away from the back wall to catch the bounce.

"Returning" to the offensive can be done in two ways: (1) either hit a winning shot off the return (kill or passing shot) or (2) hit a defensive shot that forces the server to leave the center court position. The choice of the return will usually depend on the choice of serve. A low ball (below your knees) is a prime candidate for an offensive return; a high ball above your shoulder, a defensive shot. Those balls falling in between should either be taken before dropping below shoulder level or hit after falling below the knee. Balls that rebound off the floor to the back wall should be taken after the floor bounce.

HITTING A WINNING SHOT

A shot can result in a score for one of three reasons: (1) the ball was hit so well that the opponent could not return it even though in proper court position (kill shot); (2) the ball was hit to an area of the court that the opponent could not reach in time to return the ball (passing shot); and (3) the opponent just missed the ball — an unforced error. The third reason for a score may be related to your play only if you had consistently hit for long rallies with defensive shots to tire out the opposing player. Otherwise, unforced errors must be considered as being due to a mental lapse on your opponent's part, and you cannot take credit for the point.

However, the first and second reasons for a **winning shot** depend upon your play. To hit a winning shot, you must be aggressive. Always move quickly to the ball, and align yourself correctly for the proper hit. Never wait for the ball to come to you or be satisfied with hitting the ball if it happens to be within reach if you can maneuver for a better shot.

There are three times when you can consider hitting the ball as it rebounds from the front wall (see page 20). Which you choose depends on how aggressively you are playing and whether you want to speed up or slow down the game. The first is after the ball comes off the front wall and before it hits the floor. Hitting a volley is very effective at speeding up play and possibly catching your opponent out of court position. The best return for a winning shot off a volley is a cross-court or down-the-line passing shot. Care must be taken, however, not to hit the pass so hard that the ball rebounds off the back wall into the center court playing area.

If you choose to let the ball bounce, it may be hit immediately after touching the floor as it passes between your shoelaces and knee or finally after the height of the arch is reached and the ball is falling to the floor, passing again through this same area. Aggressive players try to take most balls on the "skip," just after the floor is hit. This also works to speed up play and may catch the opponent out of court position. In addition, it offers the advantage of being at the right position from which to hit a kill shot.

Waiting until the ball arches and is falling for the second time to the floor not only gives you more time to set up for the shot, but for the opponent to set up for the return as well. Therefore, hitting the ball at this point should be primarily done by the beginning player who reacts slowly to the ball or by the experienced player who is trying to slow down the game.

Regardless of where you are when you hit the ball or what kind of ball you hit, move to cut off your opponent's anticipated return after you hit the ball. There you will be the least vulnerable to your opponent's next shot, and you can begin to set up for another winning return.

SOMETIMES A GOOD DEFENSE IS THE BEST OFFENSE

Every player will meet someone who is a match against the best serves or who can anticipate the ball's movement in the court and can score at will. Often this occurs when women play men who are more experienced court players and who, due to the speed and power of the strokes, seem to be playing in a different time zone.

The only way to make a game of this situation is to try to outmaneuver the power. This can be done in three ways: (1) slow the ball and the tempo of the game by waiting to hit the ball just before the second bounce; (2) use defensive return shots to the opponent's weak side and hit garbage serves; and (3) keep your opponent out of the center court by hitting balls wide of the midline. Trying to outgun power usually leads to a sloppy game, referred to as "Battleball" (see page 65). However, using a strategy that never gives your opponent anything "good" to hit or a court position from which to hit it eliminates the power as a factor.

Thus, the best offense for some experienced players against a power player is a good defensive game. It may not have the spark and strong rallies of a power game, but the weaker player who is the tactician will have a chance to score.

This is not to imply that the player can never hit offensive shots, but rather that these shots should only be attempted when there is a high probability of success. Indeed, the defensive game should be used to tire out the opponent by moving him/her around the court, frustrate him/her into an unforced error, or solicit a weak return that sets up your offensive shot. The name of this game is patience — patience to endure the long rallies and wait for your opening to an offensive position. Above all, to use this strategy effectively, you must be careful never to hit a low ball to your opponent's strong side, since that is just the opportunity needed to begin a power game.

Garbage serve to the backhand.

WINNING WHEN YOU ARE NOT THE BEST PLAYER

Playing the Weakness

Every player has **weakness** — a shot that the player would prefer not to hit. Your job is to find that weakness and take advantage of it if you can. If the opponent does not appear to have a weakness, create one through ball placement and court position. A player who is constantly running to hit a ball will fatigue no matter how conditioned, so keep the ball moving. If indeed the player is much stronger than you, then go for broke. Try to hit everything and anything, even the best kill shot. If you concede the shot, the point is lost; if you try for the ball, you may return just a few and stop a rally. If nothing else, Mr. Sharpshooter may think twice about the choice of hits, knowing that you came close to returning a ball. This hesitancy may cause some mis-hits and provide better opportunities for making offensive returns.

However, to have any hope that this strategy will succeed, give yourself the best chance for hitting a winner. Never hit the ball and hold court position. MOVE to cut off the return, and HUSTLE. If this strategy doesn't work, at least you put up a fight.

Points to Remember

1. Play an offensive game, plan your shots, and move your opponent around the court to set up your best return.

2. Vary your serves by changing the force of the hit, the angle off the front wall, and where the balls rebound behind the short line.

3. Anticipate your opponent's shot, and move to a court position to block it and/or set up for the return.

4. Use defensive shots from the back court position and offensive returns from a center or front court position.

5. Keep your opponent away from a center court position by hitting the balls wide of the midline of the court and into the back corners.

6. When you are tired, hit harder and move faster.

7. When playing a stronger opponent, play a defensive game and slow the tempo of play.

CHAPTER 9

Drills for the Player

Racquetball drills are useful in helping the beginning player develop the skills necessary to play the game and in giving the experienced player opportunity to practice and sharpen all shots. Drills may also be used as part of your warm-up routine to help you get the "feel" for the court and ball's movement as well as help to adjust your body to exercise.

The following list of drills was designed to provide the player with an opportunity to work on the strokes and shots used most often in a game situation. Evaluative measures are given with some drills to help you determine your proficiency with that skill and when you would be ready to incorporate it into your game plan.

The drills are listed from the most basic skills to playing modified games with an opponent. The beginning player can either start with the first drill and work through to the simulated games or pick the drills that work on the skills that are most difficult.

In all drills, starting the ball in play is critical. The ball can be either dropped or tossed against a wall. When dropped, you must be sure to drop the ball in front of your forward foot so that you can step into the stroke when contacting the ball. If the ball is tossed to a wall, position yourself so that the rebound falls in front of your body position. This will allow you to step forward to meet the ball. The wrong ball toss will result in learning to stroke at a ball that is improperly positioned in relation to your body.

SCORING SCALES

Scoring scales are presented in selected drills. The illustrations accompanying these drills indicate the size of the target area (1' or 2') and the score allotted to each target zone (5, 3, or 1 points). Balls in the targeted area can be scored by "guess,"or small pieces of masking tape can be placed on the floor and walls to outline the areas. Balls that hit a line between two point areas should be given the lower of the two scores. A legal shot not hitting the target area is scored 0 points. Although the target points are somewhat arbitrary, they do identify, through points scored, the accuracy and placement of your shots. In general, the following percentages can be used to determine the effectiveness of your returns and serves:

CATEGORY	PERCENT	USE
Excellent	90 - 100	"bread and butter" shot; use this shot whenever your strategy dictates
Good	75 - 89	consistent enough to use to vary your shots; a dependable shot in a game in which you are in control
Average	50 - 74	Be Careful — you may miss this shot half of the time; not the shot to choose when the game is close but a good shot to practice when you can afford to lose some points
Below Average	below 50	POISON! — do not hit this in a game situation because you will miss it more than half of the time

DRILLS

DRILL I

WATCHING THE GAME

Purpose: To develop a concept of how racquetball is played and the use of offensive and defensive shots during the game.

Method: Go to a court with an observation area, and watch experienced players play racquetball. Count the number of offensive and defensive shots used by each player.

DRILL II

FOREHAND SHOTS

Purpose: To practice hitting a forehand shot to the back corners of the court from three primary areas of the floor.

Method: Hit eight balls each from the mid-, center-, and back-court positions. From each position, hit four balls to the back right corner and four balls to the back left corner. Hit the ball after you've dropped it to the floor.

DRILL III

BACKHAND SHOTS

Purpose: To practice hitting a backhand shot to the back corners of the court from three primary areas of the floor.

Method: Hit eight balls each from the mid-, center-, and back-court positions. From each position, hit four balls to the back right corner and four balls to the back left corner. Hit the ball after you've dropped it to the floor.

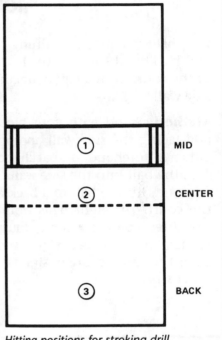

Hitting positions for stroking drill.

DRILL IV

FOREHAND AND BACKHAND SHOTS FROM SIDE-WALL TOSS

Purpose: To practice hitting forehand and backhand shots to the back corners of the court from a ball bouncing off the side wall.

Method: Stand with your hips pivoted and facing the side wall appropriate for either a forehand or backhand stroke. Toss the ball into the side wall. After the rebound, hit the ball to a back corner of the court. Hit eight balls from each of the three court positions, four to each corner, then repeat eight shots each from the same court positions with the other stroke.

Toss off the side wall.

DRILL V

SUICIDE DRILL

Purpose: To develop muscular endurance and anaerobic capacity, and to practice moving to the ball and returning it to the front wall.

Method: Begin in the center court, and after dropping the ball, hit it to the front wall. Continue to return the ball as quickly as you can, hitting all balls regardless of their court position or the number of times the ball has bounced off the floor. Work at positioning yourself correctly for each hit. Continue this drill for two minute intervals, allowing yourself to rest 30 seconds to one minute after each hitting session. Repeat the drill ten times. Record the number of balls hit each two-minute interval.

DRILL VI   30-SECOND DRILL

Purpose: To teach the player to react quickly to the ball's court position and improve his/her movement time, and to work on ball control.

Method: Begin in a center-court position. Drop the ball and return it to the front wall. Continue to return the ball off the rebound, counting the number of times the ball is returned in 30 seconds. Only count shots that would be legal returns in a game. Do this drill at least every other practice session. Try to improve one to three shots each time.

DRILL VII   SERVING DRILL — LOB AND HIGH Z

Purpose: To practice hitting lob and high Z serves correctly and accurately to a back-corner court position.

Method: Standing close to the center of the service zone, hit ten lob serves to the right back corner of the court to the designated target area. Score each serve as indicated in the diagram. Give one point to a legal serve if it lands on the correct side of the court but not into the back corner. Total the points. Refer to the scoring scale to determine the accuracy of this serve. Total points possible = 50 points. Repeat this drill with the lob serve to the left back corner and the target area. Score and evaluate. Total points = 50. (Note: for a lob hit with a backhand stroke, you may move in the service area toward the backhand side wall.) Repeat both parts of this drill using a high Z serve. Total points possible for each part = 50 points.

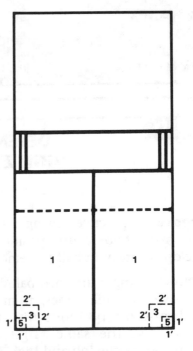

Scoring area for the lob and high Z serving drill.

Scoring Scale:	
Excellent-	45 - 50
Good-	39 - 44
Average-	25-38
Below Average-	less than 25

DRILL VIII

SERVING DRILLS — DRIVE SERVE

Purpose: To develop accuracy in your drive serve and be able to drive serve to a variety of court positions.

Method: From the center of the service zone, hit three drive serves to each of the four designated court positions. Repeat the circuit three times. Score one point for each correct placement. Total points possible = 36. (Note: you can total points scored to each designated area to indicate your most accurate placement. Total points to each area = 9.)

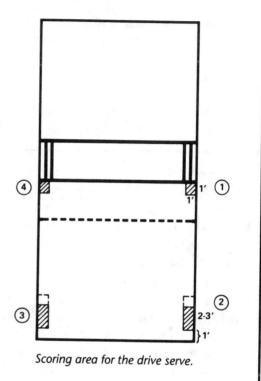

Scoring area for the drive serve.

Scoring Scale:	
Excellent-	32 - 36
Good-	27 - 31
Average-	18-26
Below Average-	less than 18

DRILL IX

DEFENSIVE SHOTS — LOB, CEILING, HIGH Z, AROUND-THE-WALL

Purpose: To practice hitting a defensive shot from two court positions and develop accuracy in ball placement.

Method: Using a dropped ball, hit each defensive shot ten times, from center- and back-court positions (five to each corner). Use the same target area as designated for the lob and high Z serves. Total points possible for each serve from each position = 50. To vary this drill, begin the defensive shot with a side wall-toss.

Scoring Scale:	
Excellent-	45 - 50
Good-	39 - 44
Average-	25 - 38
Below Average-	less than 25

DRILL X

BACK WALL DRILL

Purpose: To practice hitting balls rebounding off the back wall and accurately return them wide of the midline in a back-court area.

Method: Standing in the back court, toss balls into the back wall to rebound for a forehand stroke. Hit ten balls, returning each to the front. Score the rebound in the designated area. Total points possible = 50. Repeat the drill using a ball toss to your backhand side, and return the balls with a backhand stroke. Total points possible = 50.

Scoring Scale:	
Excellent-	45 - 50
Good-	39 - 44
Average-	25 - 38
Below Average-	less than 25

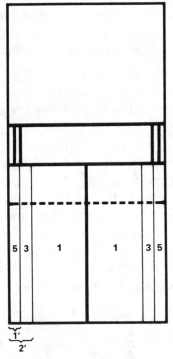

Scoring area for the back wall drill.

DRILL XI

CORNER RETURN

Purpose: To practice hitting balls after they have rebounded from a back corner and accurately return them into a back court position wide of the midline.

Method: Standing in the back court, toss a ball to your forehand side to rebound either from the back wall to a side wall or in the opposite direction. Return ten balls with your forehand stroke, then turn and toss ten balls to the opposite side/back wall for a backhand return. Hit each ball to rebound into a back-court position and wide of the midline of the court. Score each return with the same designated target area used for the back-wall returns. Total points possible for each stroke = 50.

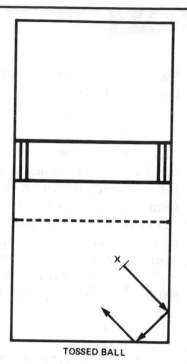

Path of a tossed ball for the corner hit drill - side wall toss.

TOSSED BALL

Scoring Scale:	
Excellent-	45 - 50
Good-	39 - 44
Average-	25 - 38
Below Average-	less than 25

Path of a tossed ball for the corner hit drill - back wall toss.

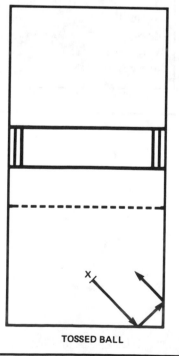

TOSSED BALL

DRILL XII

REPEAT CEILING SHOTS

Purpose: To practice hitting a ceiling return from any court position.

Method: Standing in a center-court position, use a side-wall toss to put the ball in play and hit ten consecutive ceiling returns to your forehand side without the ball hitting the floor more than once between shots. Put the ball in play again and hit ten consecutive backhand ceiling shots to the backhand side of the court. Once you are consistent with your placement, use the target area shown for Drill X and score yourself on ten forehand and ten backhand shots. Total points possible = 50.

Scoring Scale:

Excellent-	45 - 50
Good-	39 - 44
Average-	25 - 38
Below Average-	less than 25

DRILL XIII

OFFENSIVE SHOTS — PASSING

Purpose: To practice hitting passing shots from two court positions and accurately direct them to one of two court areas.

Method: Using a side-wall toss to your forehand side, hit ten passing shots from court positions A and B. Return the ball into the shaded area of the court diagram. Score one point for each successful return. Total points possible = 10. Repeat the drill using a backhand stroke. Total points possible = 10.

Scoring Scale:

Excellent-	9 - 10
Good-	7 - 8
Average-	5 - 6
Below Average-	less than 5

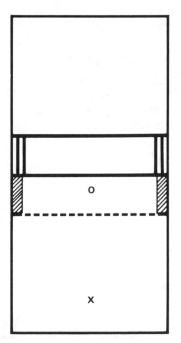

A. Target area for a passing shot for a back court position.

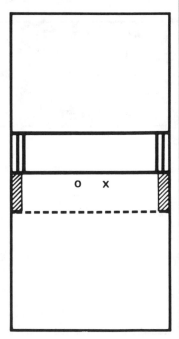

B. Target area for a passing shot from a center court position.

DRILL XIV

OFFENSIVE SHOTS — KILL

Purpose: To practice hitting accurate kill shots from three court positions.

Method: Dropping the ball to your forehand side, hit ten kill shots from each court position: A, B, and C. Score each position separately using a front-wall target area. Use corner and pinch kill shots. Total points possible = 50. Repeat the drill using a drop to your backhand side. Total points possible = 50 from each court position. This drill can also be varied by using a side-wall toss to put the ball in play.

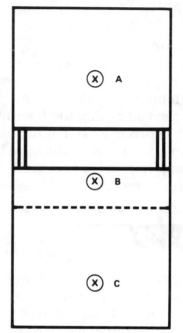

Hitting positions for the kill shot drill.

Scoring Scale:	
Excellent-	45 - 50
Good-	39 - 44
Average-	25 - 38
Below Average-	less than 25

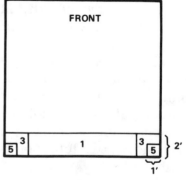

Scoring area for the kill shot drill.

DRILL XV

RALLY DRILL — HIT AND MOVE

Purpose: To practice hitting a ball and moving away from the rebound to avoid colliding with your opponent on the court.

Method: Standing side by side in the back court with your opponent, the player on the right side of the court hits a ball straight into the front wall. After hitting, this player moves to the left and out of the way of the opponent moving toward the ball. The ball is again returned straight into the front wall, and the positions are again reversed. Continue this rotation until the ball is missed.

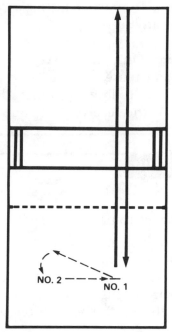

Rally drill to avoid collisions on the court.

DRILL XVI

MINI-GAME

Purpose: To give players a chance to practice serving and returning the serve.

Method: Each player serves five times and then rotates to the back court to be the receiver. The game is to 15 points, and a point is scored by either player on each rally regardless of whether he/she was serving.

DRILL XVII

DEFENSIVE RETURN GAME

Purpose: To practice hitting a defensive shot off any serve.

Method: Only the server scores. The server must use a drive serve and the receiver a ceiling or other defensive return. If the receiver does not use this type of return, the server scores a point. If the drive serve is not hit, a side out occurs. Variation: change the type of serve required to be hit, or specify exactly which defensive shot needs to be returned.

DRILL XVIII

GAME WARM-UP DRILL

Purpose: To provide a method for warming up before a game.

Method: Begin by standing side by side with your opponent just behind the short line. Practice hitting forehand strokes to the front wall. After several minutes, move two-thirds of the way back to the back wall and practice ceiling shots from this position. Finally, back up to the back wall and hit offensive and defensive returns to the front wall from a ball toss off the back wall.

Players warming up before a game.

CHAPTER 10

Court Etiquette and Interpreting the Rules

As in all sport activities, there is a degree of courtesy involved in a competitive racquetball game, and there is a great need to understand and interpret the rules of the game in a fair and objective manner. With two individuals enclosed in a space of 20' x 20' x 40', there is little room for disagreement. The possibility of injury and negative feelings increases if every courtesy is not extended to the opponent and if the rules are not complied with in detail.

PRIOR TO THE START

Prior to the start of the match, the court must be shared by players executing the shots to be used in the match. In that warm-up each player needs to control ball placement to avoid interference with the opponent. The court should be divided in length, and all shots should be hit within that boundary. During the warm-up, players should only hit shots they can control, and they should be considerate if the

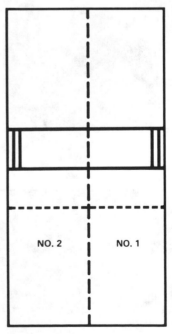

NO. 2   NO. 1

Court divided in length for warm-up.

Two players warming up side by side.

Stopping execution of a warm-up shot when a player walks in front of another player.

opponent retrieves a ball into the front of the court. Stopping execution of a shot if the opponent walks in front of you or moves to your court to retrieve a ball are specific examples. Bouncing the ball back to the opponent is also appreciated and in good taste.

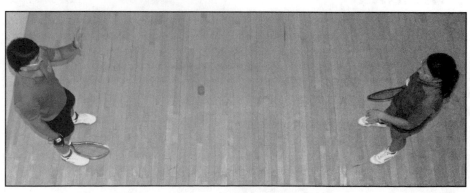

Bouncing the ball back to an opponent when warming up.

SCORING, SERVING, AND BALL IN PLAY

Use of proper etiquette and interpretation of the rules during the game is crucial to acceptable play. Some of the rules are quite simple, yet the beginning player sometimes does not initially respond to the obvious and needs to be informed of a rule that most experienced players take for granted.

Legal position of the server in relation to the serving zone.

Scoring

How to keep score is one of those rules that is taken for granted, yet should be explained. A game is won when the first player reaches 15 points; thus, a score of 15-14 is a legal game. To win a match in most situations requires you to win the best of three games. If each player has won one game, the third game is played to 11 points, again with the need to win only by one point (i.e., 11-10 is a legal score). In class situations, students may discover that games are played to an assortment of final points to accommodate class procedure.

Serving

There are specific **rules governing the service** in racquetball. First, the server must stand between the short line and service line — an area commonly called the service zone. The back foot of the server must be inside the short line and neither foot is allowed to step fully over the service line. The service zone is defined as the back of the paint of the short line and the front of the service line paint. To initiate a serve, the player must drop the ball and then strike it with the racquet after the ball rebounds off the floor. Following racquet contact on the serve, the ball must strike the front wall first on the fly and then carry beyond the short line. The ball must strike the floor beyond the short line before hitting the back wall, ceiling, or more than one side wall. A screen serve, an illegal drive serve, and a serve that strikes the front wall on the fly and doesn't carry beyond the short line are fault serves. Serves that hit two or more side walls, the back wall on the fly, and the ceiling on the fly are also described as **fault** serves. Common terms for a fault include a **short** for a serve that doesn't carry past the short line, a **long** for a ball that hits the back wall on the fly, **two walls** for a serve that hits more than one side wall on the fly.

The fault serve mentioned above as an illegal drive serve deserves special mention. There are two drive serve lines, each three feet from the side wall located in the service zone. The server may drive serve to

Drive serve box.

the same side of the court that the serve is initiated as long as the start and finish of the server's serve motion takes place outside of the three foot drive serve zone. A second serve opportunity is provided following all fault serves.

An **out** serve signifies the loss of serve. Loss of serve occurs when the ball does not hit the front wall on the fly after the server hits the ball, or when two faults are served in succession. There are additional out serves including: a missed serve attempt, a crotch serve off the front wall, and a serve striking a partner who is standing outside the doubles box in a doubles match.

Calling the score prior to every serve is expected in a racquetball match. The server's score is always called first, alerting your opponent that the score is agreed to by both parties unless the opponent stops play to question it. Also, calling the score implies that the next serve is going to follow shortly, and the opponent should be ready to receive.

Ball in Play

Once the **ball is in play**, it must be hit by each of the players (in singles) alternately. The ultimate goal of either player is to hit the ball so it strikes the front wall before hitting the floor. A ball can hit the back wall, followed by the ceiling and side walls, as long as it eventually gets to the front wall before touching the floor.

A server continues the serve for each point played until two faults are hit in succession, an out serve is made, or the server cannot return the opponent's shot in a legal manner (i.e., not returning the ball to the front wall before it strikes the floor, hitting after the second bounce, or committing a point hinder). A return-of-serve player remains in that situation until the serving opponent has made one of the above-mentioned errors.

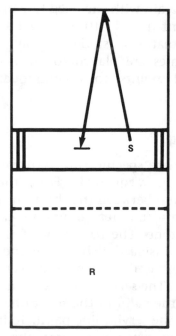

Short serve fault.

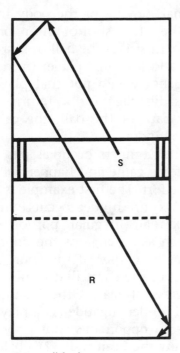

Two wall fault.

HINDERS

Hinders need to be discussed in detail when interpreting the rules. There are two basic types of hinders in racquetball. The **avoidable hinders** are usually intentional acts of preventing an opponent from a fair try at hitting the ball. **Dead ball hinders**, commonly called hinders, occur by accident of court play but also are associated with preventing the opponent from having a fair chance at the ball.

Avoidable hinders are usually called on a player who intentionally moves in the path of an opponent to prevent the opponent from hitting the ball or seeing it clearly. Experienced players are quite skilled at committing avoidable hinders called **blocking**. The player committing the infraction may hit a shot from an "up"

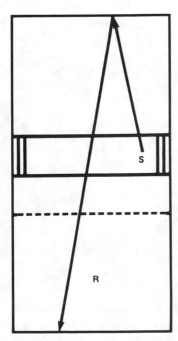

Long serve fault.

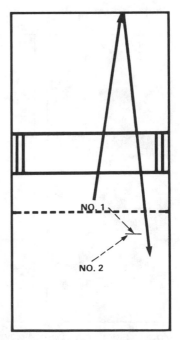

Blocking of an opponent in the back court: avoidable hinder.

position and then set up to block the movement of the opponent in a "back" position. The movement is subtle and discourages the opponent from making an attempt to reach the ball, since the opponent is in a "back" position. There are countless avoidable hinders in racquetball. The player who simply will not move to permit an opponent access to the ball is one example. A second example is a player who will move next to an opponent attempting a full-swing shot. That opponent will not be able to complete the swing because of the position of the other player. A third example is a player pushing or shoving an opponent as a means of gaining impetus to move to reach a ball. Pushing off an opponent gives an unfair advantage, since it may place the opponent in an off-balance position for the next shot. A fourth distinct violation associated with avoidable hinders is the

intentional moving of the body into the path of the return shot of an opponent. If an opponent strikes the ball from a "back" position and the "up" player (recognizing that the shot would put that player at a great disadvantage for a return) moves into the path of the ball, the call is an avoidable hinder.

Dead ball hinders occur as part of the action of the game and happen without a planned effort. The first example is a court hinder. A court hinder occurs when the ball strikes an irregular portion of the court, such as an edge of the door, a can placed in the corner of the court, or any other part of the court that would impede the progress of play. Other examples of dead ball hinders include (1) a player who is hit by an opponent's shot prior to the ball striking the front wall; (2) a ball that is "shadowed" so that the opponent cannot see the ball clearly; and (3) a ball that goes

A Player who doesn't move out of the way: avoidable hinder.

A player moving too close to a player attempting a shot: avoidable hinder.

A player pushing an opponent to get a ball: avoidable hinder.

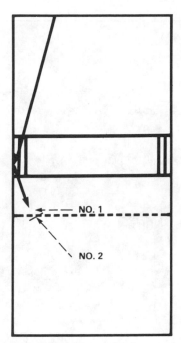

Moving into the path of an
opponent, creating a hinder:
avoidable hinder.

The ball hitting a ball can: dead ball hinder.

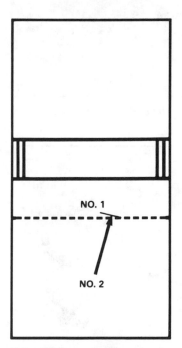

*Being hit by an opponent's
shot: dead ball hinder.*

Edge of door: dead ball hinder.

between the legs of the opponent, thus distracting the player hitting the ball. In addition, when two players collide attempting to move out of the way of each other or the ball, or attempting to reach the ball, play is stopped and a hinder is called.

Shadowing the ball: dead ball hinder.

Two players colliding: dead ball hinder.

A straddle ball: dead ball hinder.

The etiquette of calling a dead ball hinder rests initially with the player who creates the problem. That player's obligation is to state, "Do you want a hinder?" The response from the other player is either "Yes" or "No." If a hinder is identified by the offending player, the player restricted may say "Hinder please," and the opposing player has only the choice of "Okay." In short, any request for a hinder is to be honored in an immediate affirmative manner. Hinders are to be requested immediately following the infraction so that no question arises concerning whether or not a hinder should be called.

An avoidable hinder results in a point loss to the opponent if the opponent was receiving and committed the infraction, and a side out if the infraction was made by the server. A dead ball hinder requires a replay of the point. In a "friendly" game, point hinders should seldom happen, since the idea of the game is to play for enjoyment and fitness. If a player does resort to committing avoidable hinders in such an environment, a judicial response is to not play that person again.

MISCELLANEOUS RULES

The necessary rules interpretations include the use of the racquet. Often, beginners are not aware that the racquet must be held in one hand and remain in that hand throughout any specific rally. The racquet must also be attached to the wrist by the thong in order to reduce the possibility of injury. Another interpretation that is common knowledge, but that often is misunderstood, is that the ball must always be struck only by the racquet for a legal return. Other commonly misunderstood rules include the following:

1. The ball must be dry before being placed in play.
2. A server may not take a running stride to execute the serve.
3. A receiver of serve may not cross the receiving line until the served ball has crossed the short line, thus eliminating a potentially hazardous situation. The **receiving five-foot line** is marked by a three-inch vertical

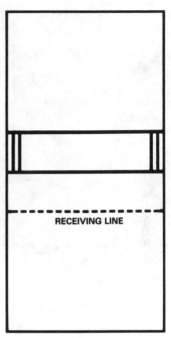

Five foot receiving line.

line placed on each side wall directly behind the short-line position extended from one side wall to the other.

4. A **crotch shot** strikes the floor and a wall simultaneously. During a serve, a crotch shot off the front wall is an out serve. A crotch shot serve that strikes off the back wall is in play. During play, a crotch shot is always in play unless it hits the front wall.

5. Only the server is permitted to score after a winning rally.

Understanding the common rules of serving, hinders, and scoring allows the novice freedom to play the game early in skill development.

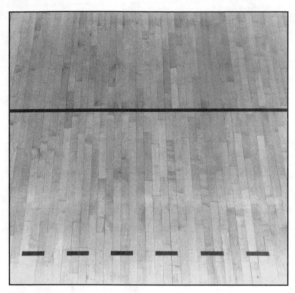

Receiving line.

Vertical line describing the five foot receiving line.

DOUBLES AND CUTTHROAT

The singles match in a racquetball is the only game recommended for safe, enjoyable play, but there are two other games associated with racquetball and rules interpretation. One is called **doubles** and should, if possible, be played on a regulation doubles court that is larger than a traditional singles court. The other game, played with three players, is called **cutthroat**.

Doubles

Rules that relate to doubles are distinct in some ways, including serving order, player hitting order, position during serve, and hinder situations. The serve order follows a sequence of one partner serving consecutive points until a side out occurs, and then the second partner serving in a similar fashion until a second side out takes place. There is one exception to the service order of the partners, and that fits only the first serving team. The first partner serves to the conclusion of serve, then the team exchanges with the receiving team. When the first serving team returns for the second round of serves, the first serving partner again begins serve, followed by the normal sequence of partner serve rotation. The player-hitting order, once the ball is placed in play by a serve, is the same as in the singles game, with team A hitting a serve, team B returning the serve, team A responding to return of

Doubles serving position.

serve, etc. Either player on a team may hit for that team in the rally.

During a serve, the serving team stands within the service zone as in the singles play experience. One partner serves, and the other partner is directed to stand in the service box with his/her back to the side wall or a foot-fault is called. If the partner in the doubles box is struck by the partner's serve, the serve is declared "dead," and the serve is executed again. Once the ball is in play, any ball that is hit by one partner that strikes the other partner is deemed a side out or a loss of point, depending on whether the serving or receiving team committed the infraction. The receiving team must stand behind the receiving line to receive serve. Hinders are the same as in singles play, but the possibility for hinder calls is magnified by the presence of four players on the court at one time.

Cutthroat

The cutthroat game is an unofficial racquetball game with a safety feature built in. One cutthroat game is a two-against-one setup, with the receiving team playing as a doubles team, and the serving player competing against that team. Following each side out, the doubles team membership changes, and the server becomes a part of a new doubles team. All play on the part of the doubles team as related to movement and position utilizes doubles rules, and all other play commences as in singles. The serving rotation follows a sequence of the server as the number-one player exchanging with the

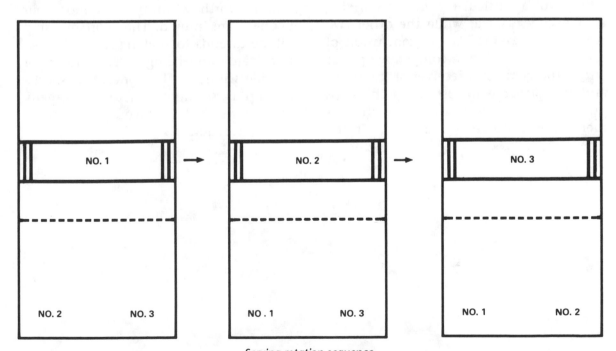

Serving rotation sequence.

number-two player, who is a receiver. When the next side out occurs, the number-two player, who has been the server, exchanges with the number-three player, who is the second receiver. The sequence follows an exchange with the number-three player (who is the server) on the next side out with the number-one player, who has moved through the sequence as receiver. Then the process is repeated. It should be noted that this type of exchange alternates the position of the receiver each time through the full serving sequence. If the number-two receiver started from a right-side receiving position during the first sequence, that number-two player would receive from the left side during the second sequence of return of serve.

The second type of cutthroat game is a safer version and becomes a singles match with three players. One player is always sitting out a particular point by standing in a back-wall area, while the other two players are playing. At the conclusion of each point, the non-competing player enters the game as a receiver of the serve, and the player who lost the point steps out. If the server loses the point, the former receiver becomes the server. If the receiver loses the point, the server remains as server, and play continues. In both games of cutthroat, each player keeps an individual score, and the winner is the first player to gain 15 points. The game of cutthroat provides for a change-of-pace situation that permits three people to enjoy a game designed for two or four.

SPORTSMANSHIP ETHIC

Racquetball has a **sportsmanship ethic** that implies that the game is played for exercise and enjoyment. Coupled with that implication is the view that most matches are played without officiating, and it is imperative to call each point or shot fairly and without prejudice. It is doubly important to recognize that no point is worth winning if you or your opponent are injured. The sportsmanship attitude extends to shaking hands following a match and being a "good loser" or "humble winner." The concept of sportsmanship is so much rhetoric in many other sports, but in racquetball, sportsmanship is required.

Glossary

Ace: A legal serve that is totally missed by the receiver of the serve.

Around-the-wall ball: A defensive shot that hits three walls before touching the floor.

Avoidable Hinder: Interference with the opponent's opportunity to play a shot fairly that includes: failure to move, stroke interference, blocking, moving into the ball, pushing, intentional distractions, view obstruction, and wetting of the ball.

Back Court: That section of the court nearest the back wall and described as the last third of the court.

Backhand: A stroke hit from the non-racquet side of the body.

Backswing: The preparation phase of the basic swing.

Ceiling Shot: A ball that strikes ceiling-front wall or front wall-ceiling in sequence.

Center Court: The area immediately behind the short-line and equal distance from the side walls.

Closed Face: Position of the racquet face on the ball when hitting the ball downward, (i.e., usually turned away from the ceiling).

Continental Grip: The grip positioned halfway between the Eastern forehand and the backhand grip.

Corner Kill Shot: A kill shot that strikes the front wall-side wall and rebounds into the direction of mid court.

Cross-Court Shot: A two-wall passing shot executed when the opponent is either on the same side as you or is in an "up" position. The ball hits front wall and then side wall.

Crotch: A ball that strikes two playing surfaces simultaneously.

Cutthroat: A three-player racquetball game designed with the server playing against the other two players.

Dead Ball Hinder: An unintentional interference with the opponent's opportunity to play a shot fairly, including: court hinders, ball hitting an opponent, body contact, screen ball, backswing hinder, and a safety hold up.

Defensive Shots: Shots that prevent the opponent from holding an offensive court position.

Doubles: A four-player racquetball game played between teams of two players.

Down-the-line Passing Shot: A shot that carries along a side wall one to two feet from the wall and below the opponent's waist. This is also called down-the-wall and it is designed to pass an opponent who is in an "up" position.

Drive Serve Zone: The zone defined by two lines three feet from each side wall in the service box that divides the service zone into two seventeen foot service zones for drive serves. The zone is associated with the special rule regarding drive serves.

Eastern Forehand Grip: The conventional racquetball grip that is best described as a "shake hands" position.

Eastern Backhand Grip: The conventional backhand grip that is assumed by rotating the racquet a quarter turn to the racquet side of the body from the Eastern Forehand grip.

Fault: A serve that touches the floor before passing the short line or one in which the ball strikes the front wall and either the ceiling, the back wall, or two side walls before hitting the floor. These serves are illegal and must be replayed. Two faults result in a side out.

Forehand: A stroke hit from the racquet side of the body.

Front Court: That section of the court in front of the service line.

Front Wall Kill: A kill shot that hits the front wall straight on and rebounds toward the back wall without touching a side wall.

Garbage Serve: A serve hit between the speed of a drive and lob serve that bounces between the shoulder and waist to the receiver. The serve gives an illusion of a miss-hit serve.

High Z Serve: A serve that strikes high off the front wall (near the ceiling) and follows a "Z" pattern across the court.

Hinder: Any situation that prevents an opponent from having a fair shot at hitting the ball during a rally. Hinders include avoidable and dead ball hinders.

Kill Shot: Any ball that strikes the front wall hard and low so that the rebound with the floor occurs almost simultaneously with the wall. A winning offensive shot.

Lob: A defensive shot, hit along a side wall so that it follows a path high over center court and falls with little rebound into a back corner. This ball may touch a side wall close to the back corner.

Long: A serve that strikes the back wall on the fly. A fault.

Match: The culmination of a competition with the winner usually winning two of three games.

Mid Court: The area between the service and short line and the two side walls.

Non-Thinking Strategy: Following a defensive reactive strategy with few decisions to make.

Offensive Shot: The attempt to win a point outright by virtue of the skill with which the shot is hit.

"On Edge": The position of the racquet face when it is perpendicular to the floor.

Open Face: Position of the racquet face on the ball when hitting the ball up (i.e., usually turned toward the ceiling).

Overhead: Shots hit from above the shoulder position with an extended arm.

Overhead Kill: A kill shot hit off a ball positioned above the shoulder.

Over-the-Shoulder: A ball hit from a position directly over the shoulder.

Passing Shot: An offensive shot that literally goes past an opponent who is in the front-, mid-, or center-court positions.

Pinch Kill: A shot that strikes the side wall-front wall sequence and that is unreturnable due to the low position, high velocity of the shot. Also called a pinch shot.

Protective Eyewear: Safety glasses required for wear when entering a racquetball court.

Racquet Face: The portion of the racquet with which the ball is struck during play.

Rally: A continuous exchange of shots during the play of a point.

Receiving Line: The line identified by the intermittent floor marks located five feet behind the short line. A player may not stand in front of the receiving line to receive a serve.

"Run the Corner": A ball that rebounds to a back corner, hitting the side wall and back wall before striking the floor.

Screen: A blocking of the opponent's vision, preventing the opponent from seeing the ball.

Service Line: The line on the floor closest to the front wall. The front line of the service zone.

Service Zone: The area between the service line and the short line. The area of the court for the server to legally execute the serve.

Set: The ready position. The position that enables the receiver of a shot to turn or pivot to hit the ball.

Set Up: A ball that is hit so the opponent can easily return it.

Short: A served ball that touches the floor in front of or on the short line. A fault.

Short Line: The line on the floor nearest the back wall. The back line of the service zone.

Side Out: A loss of a serve to the opponent.

Thong: The safety strap that is attached to the racquet grip and worn around the wrist.

Thinking Strategy: The act of taking advantage of an opponent through the use of intellect, court strategy, and skill.

Three-Wall Shot: A defensive shot that rebounds off three walls.

Volley: Striking the ball in midair from a rebound off the front wall before the ball touches the floor.

Wallpaper Shot: A ball that rebounds along a side wall, making a return extremely difficult.

Western Grip: A grip that is used for a forehand stroke. It is similar to the grip used on a racquet when it is picked up off the floor.

1990-91
Official Rules

1 — THE GAME

Rule 1.1. TYPES OF GAMES

Racquetball may be played by two or four players. When played by two it is called singles and when played by four, doubles. A non-tournament variation of the game that is played by three players is called cut-throat.

Rule 1.2. DESCRIPTION

Racquetball is a competitive game in which a racquet is used to serve and return the ball.

Rule 1.3. OBJECTIVE

The objective is to win each rally by serving or returning the ball so the opponent is unable to keep the ball in play. A rally is over when a player (or team in doubles), makes an error, is unable to return the ball before it touches the floor twice, or when a hinder is called.

Rule 1.4. POINTS AND OUTS

Points are scored only by the serving side when it serves an ace (an irretrievable serve) or wins a rally. Losing the serve is called an out in singles. In doubles, when the first server loses serve it is called a *handout* and when the second server loses the serve it is a *sideout*.

Rule 1.5. MATCH, GAME, TIEBREAKER

A match is won by the first side winning two games. The first two games of a match are played to 15 points. In the event each side wins one game, the tiebreaker game is played to 11 points.

Rule 1.6. DOUBLES TEAM

(a) A doubles team shall consist of two players who meet either the age requirements or player classification requirements to participate in a particular division of play. A team with different skill levels must play in the division of the player with the higher level of ability. When playing in an adult age division, the team must play in the division of the younger player. When playing in a junior age division, the team must play in the division of the older player.

(b) A change in playing partners may be made so long as the first match of the posted team has not begun. For this purpose only the match will be considered started once the teams have been called to the court: The team must notify the tournament director of the change prior to the beginning of the match.

Rule 1.7. CONSOLATION MATCHES

(a) Each entrant shall be entitled to participate in a minimum of two matches. Therefore, losers of their first match shall have the opportunity to compete in a consolation bracket of their own division. In draws of less than seven players, a round robin may be offered. See Rule 5.5 for determining round robin scoring.

(b) Consolation matches may be waived at the discretion of the tournament director, but this waiver must be in writing on the tournament application.

Reprinted with permission of the American Amateur Racquetball Association, Colorado Springs, Colorado

(c) Preliminary consolation matches will be two of three games to 11 points. Semifinal and final matches will follow the regular scoring format.

2 — COURTS AND EQUIPMENT

Rule 2.1. COURTS

The specifications for the standard four-wall racquetball court are:

(a) **Dimensions.** The dimensions shall be 20 feet wide, 40 feet long and 20 feet high with a back wall at least 12 feet high. All surfaces shall be in play, with the exception of any gallery opening or surfaces designated as court hinders.

(b) **Lines and Zones.** Racquetball courts shall be divided and marked with lines 1½ inches wide as follows:

(1) **Short Line.** The back edge of the short line is midway between, and is parallel with, the front and back walls.

(2) **Service Line.** The front edge of the service line is parallel with, and five feet in front of, the back edge of the short line.

(3) **Service Zone.** The service zone is the five-foot area between the outer edges of the short line and service line.

(4) **Service Boxes.** The service boxes are located at each end of the service zone and are designated by lines parallel with the side walls. The edge of the line nearest to the center of the court shall be 18 inches from the nearest side wall.

(5) **Drive Serve Lines.** The drive serve lines, which form the drive serve zone, are parallel with the side wall and are within the service zone. The edge of the line nearest to the center of the court shall be three feet from the nearest side wall.

(6) **Receiving Line.** The receiving line is a broken line parallel to the short line. The back edge of the receiving line is five feet from the back edge of the short line. The receiving line begins with a line 21 inches long that extends from each side wall: the two lines are connected by an alternate series of six-inch spaces and six-inch lines (17 six-inch spaces and 16 six-inch lines.)

(7) **Safety Zone.** The safety zone is the five-foot area bounded by the back edges of the short line and the receiving line. The zone is observed only during the serve. (See Rules 4.11.(k) and 4.12.)

Rule 2.2. BALL SPECIFICATIONS

(a) The standard racquetball shall be 2¼ inches in diameter; weight approximately 1.4 ounces; have a hardness of 55-60 inches durometer; and bounce 68-72 inches from a 100-inch drop at a temperature of 70-74 degrees Fahrenheit.

(b) Only a ball having the endorsement or approval of the AARA may be used in an AARA-sanctioned event.

Rule 2.3. BALL SELECTION

(a) A ball shall be selected by the referee for use in each match. During the match the referee may, at his discretion or at the request of a player or team, replace the ball. Balls that are not round or which bounce erratically shall not be used.

(b) If possible, the referee and players should agree to an alternate ball, so that in the event of breakage, the second ball can be put into play immediately.

Rule 2.4. RACQUET SPECIFICATIONS

(a) The racquet, including bumper guard and all solid parts of the handle, may not exceed 21 inches in length. **NOTE: Until June 1, 1991, racquets longer than 21 inches that do not exceed 21.5 inches in length may be used except in AARA Regional and National events.**

(b) The racquet frame may be of any material judged to be safe.

(c) The racquet frame must include a thong that must be securely attached to the player's wrist.

(d) The string of the racquet should be gut, monofilament, nylon, graphite, plastic, metal, or a combination thereof, providing the strings do not mark or deface the ball.

Rule 2.5. APPAREL

(a) **Lensed Eyewear Required.** Lensed eyewear designed for racquet sports is required apparel for all players. The protective eyewear must be worn as designed and may not be altered. Players who require corrective eyewear also must wear lensed eyewear designed for racquet sports. (**NOTE:** An updated list of lensed eyewear is available by writing the AARA national office. The AARA recommends that players select eyewear with polycarbonate plastic lenses with 3-mm center thickness.) Failure to wear protective eyewear will result in a technical and the player will be charged with a timeout to secure eyewear. The second infraction in the same match will result in a forfeit. (See Rule 4.18.(a)(9).)

(b) **Clothing and Shoes.** The clothing may be of any color; however, a player may be required to change extremely loose fitting or otherwise distracting garments. Insignias and writing on the clothing must be considered to be in good taste by the tournament director. Shoes must have soles which do not mark or damage the floor.

3 — OFFICIATING

Rule 3.1. TOURNAMENT MANAGEMENT

All AARA-sanctioned tournaments shall be managed by a tournament director, who shall designate the officials.

Rule 3.2. TOURNAMENT RULES COMMITTEE

The tournament director may appoint a tournament rules committee to resolve any disputes that the referee, match control desk, or tournament director cannot resolve. The committee should consist of an odd number of qualified persons who should be prepared to meet on short notice, if required. If possible, this committee should include the state director or a designated representative and any other qualified individuals, such as regional or national officers, in attendance. The tournament director should NOT be a member of this committee.

Rule 3.3. REFEREE APPOINTMENT AND REMOVAL

The principal official for every match shall be the referee who has been designated by the tournament director, or his designated representative, and who has been agreed upon by all participants in the match. The referee may be removed from a match upon the agreement of all participants (teams in doubles) or at the discretion of the tournament director or his designated representative. In the event that a referee's removal is requested by one player or team and not agreed to by the other, the tournament director or his designated representative may accept or reject the request. It is suggested that the match be observed before determining what, if any, action is to be taken. In addition, two line judges and a scorekeeper may also be designated to assist the referee in officiating the match.

Rule 3.4. RULE BRIEFING

Before all tournaments, all officials and players shall be briefed on rules and on local court hinders, regulations and modifications the tournament director wishes to impose. The briefing should be reduced to writing. The current AARA rules will apply and be made available. Any modifications the tournament director wishes to impose must be stated on the entry form and be available to all players at registration.

Rule 3.5. REFEREES

(a) **Pre-Match Duties.** Before each match begins, it shall be the duty of the referee to:

(1) Check on adequacy of preparation of court with respect to cleanliness, lighting and temperature.

(2) Check on availability and suitability of materials — to include balls, towels, scorecards, pencils and timepiece — necessary for the match.

(3) Check the readiness and qualifications of the line judges and scorekeeper. Review appeal procedure and instruct them of their duties, rules and local regulations.

(4) Go on the court to introduce himself and the players; brief the players on court hinders, local regulations, rule modifications for this tournament; explain misinterpreted rules.

(5) Inspect players' equipment, point out line judges; verify selection of a primary and alternate ball.

(6) Toss coin and allow winner choice of serving or receiving.

(b) **Decisions.** During the match, the referee shall make all decisions with regard to the rules. Where line judges are used, the referee shall announce all final judgments. If both players in singles and three out of four in a doubles match disagree with a call made by the referee, the referee is overruled.

(c) **Protests.** Any decision not involving the judgment of the referee will, on protest, be accorded due process as set forth in the By-Laws of the AARA. For the purposes of rendering a prompt decision regarding protests filed during the course of an on-going tournament, the stages of due process will be first to the tournament director and second to the tournament rules committee. In those instances when time permits, the protest may be elevated to the state association and then to the national board of directors in the manner prescribed in the By-Laws.

(d) **Forfeitures.** A match may be forfeited by the referee when:

(1) Any player refuses to abide by the referee's decision or engages in unsportsmanlike conduct.

(2) Any player or team who fails to report to play 10 minutes after the match has been scheduled to play. (The tournament director may permit a longer delay if circumstances warrant such a decision.)

(e) **Defaults.** A player or team may be forfeited by the tournament director or official for failure to comply with the tournament or host facility's rules while on the premises between matches, or for abuse of hospitality, locker room, or other rules and procedures.

(f) **Spectators.** The referee shall have jurisdiction over the spectators, as well as the players, while the match is in progress.

(g) **Other Rulings.** The referee may rule on all matters not covered in the AARA Official Rulebook. However, the referee's ruling is subject to protest as described in Rule 3.5(c).

Rule 3.6. LINE JUDGES

(a) **When Utilized.** Two line judges should be selected for all semifinal and final matches, when requested by a player or team, or when the referee or tournament director so desires. However, the use of line judges is subject to availability and the discretion of the tournament director.

(b) **Replacing Line Judges.** If any player objects to the selection of a line judge before the match begins, all reasonable effort shall be made to find a replacement acceptable to the officials and players. If a player objects to a line judge after the match begins, any replacement shall be at the discretion of the referee and/or tournament director.

(c) **Position of Judges.** The players and referee shall designate the court location of the line judges. Any dispute shall be settled by the tournament director.

(d) **Duties and Responsibilities.** Line judges are designated to help decide appealed calls. In the event of an appeal, and after a very brief explanation of the appeal by the referee, the line judges must indicate their opinion of the referee's call.

(e) **Signals.** The signal to show agreement with the referee is arm extended with *thumbs up*, disagreement is *thumbs down*. The signal to show no opinion or that the disputed play wasn't seen is open *palm down*.

(f) **Manner of Response.** Line judges should be careful not to signal until the referee acknowledges the appeal and asks for a ruling. In responding to the referee's request, line judges should not look at each other, but indicate their opinions simultaneously in clear view of the players and referee. If at any time a line judge is unsure of which call is being appealed or what the referee's call was, the line judge should ask the referee to repeat the call and the appeal.

(g) **Result of Response.** If both line judges signal no opinion, the referee's call stands. If both line judges disagree with the referee, the referee must reverse the ruling. If one line judge agrees with the call and one disagrees, the referee's call stands. If one line judge agrees with the call and one has no opinion, the call stands. If one line judge disagrees with the referee's call and the other signals no opinion, the rally is replayed. Any replays, with the exception of appeals on the second serve itself, will result in two serves.

Rule 3.7. APPEALS

(a) **Appealable Calls and Non-calls.** In any match using line judges, a player may appeal only the following calls or non-calls by the referee: kill shots; skip balls; fault serves, except screen serves; out serves; double bounce pickups; receiving line violations; and court hinders. At no time may a player appeal a screen serve, a hinder call (except court hinders), a technical foul, or other discretionary call of the referee.

(b) **How to Appeal.** A verbal appeal by a player must be made directly to the referee immediately after the rally has ended. A player who believes there is an infraction to appeal, should bring it to the attention of the referee and line judges by raising his non-racquet hand at the point of the serve or rally where the infraction occurred. The player is obligated to continue to play until the rally has ended or the referee stops play. The referee will recognize a player's appeal only if it is made before that player leaves the court for any reason including timeouts and game-ending rallies or, if that player doesn't leave the court, before the next serve begins.

(c) **Loss of Appeal.** A player or team forfeits its right of appeal for that rally if the appeal is made directly to the line judges or, if the appeal is made after an excessive demonstration or complaint.

(d) **Limit on Appeals.** A player or team may make three appeals per game. However, if either line judge disagrees with the referee's call, that appeal will not count against the three-appeal limit. In addition, the game-ending rally may be appealed even if the three-appeal limit has been reached.

Rule 3.8. OUTCOME OF APPEALS

(a) **Kill Shot and Skip Ball.** If the referee makes a call of *good* on a kill shot, pinch or pass attempt, the loser may appeal. If the call is reversed, the side which originally lost the rally is declared the winner. If the referee makes a call of *skip ball* on a pass, pinch, or kill shot attempt, that call also may be appealed. If the call is reversed, the referee then must decide if the shot could have been returned had play continued. If in the opinion of the referee, the shot could not have been returned, the rally shall be replayed. If the shot was not retrievable, the side which originally lost the rally is declared the winner.

(b) **Fault Serve.** If the referee makes a call of *fault* on a serve, the server may appeal. If the call is reversed, the serve is replayed, except: if the referee considered the serve an ace (not retrievable), a point is awarded to the server. If the referee makes no call on a serve (which indicated the serve was good), either side may appeal. If the non-call is reversed, it will result in second serve, or loss of serve if the infraction occurred on the second serve.

(c) **Out Serve.** If the referee makes a call of *out serve*, the server may appeal. If the call is reversed, the serve will be replayed. If the call is reversed and the serve is considered an ace, a point will be awarded.

(d) **Double-Bounce Pickup.** If the referee makes a call of *two bounces*, play stops and the side against whom the call was made may appeal. If the call is reversed, the rally is replayed, except: if the player against whom the call was made hits a shot that could not be retrieved, that player wins the rally. (Before awarding a rally in that situation, the referee must be certain that the shot would not have been retrieved even if play had not been halted.)

(e) **Receiving Line Violation (Encroachment).** If the referee makes a call of encroachment thereby stopping the play, the receiving side may appeal the call. If the appeal is successful, the service shall be replayed, except: if in the opinion of the referee the shot was not retrievable it will result in a loss of serve. If the referee makes no call and the server feels there was encroachment, the server may appeal. If the appeal is successful the service results in a point. (For safety zone violations by the server or doubles partner, see Rule 4.11.(k).)

(f) **Court Hinder.** If the referee makes a call of court *hinder*, play is stopped and the rally is replayed. If the referee makes no call and a player feels that a court hinder occurred, that player may appeal. If the appeal is successful, the rally will be replayed.

Rule 3.9. RULES INTERPRETATIONS

If a player feels the referee has interpreted the rules incorrectly, the player may require the referee or tournament director to show him the applicable rule in the rulebook. Having discovered a misapplication or misinterpretation, the official must correct the error by replaying the rally, awarding the point, calling sideout or taking whatever corrective measure necessary.

4 — PLAY REGULATIONS

Rule 4.1. SERVE

The player or team winning the coin toss has the option to serve or receive for the start of the first game. The second game will begin in reverse order of the first game. The player or team scoring the highest total of points in games 1 and 2 will have the option to serve or receive first at the start of the tiebreaker. In the event that both players or teams score an equal number of points in the first two games, another coin toss will take place and the winner of the toss will have the option to serve or receive.

Rule 4.2. START

The server may not start the service motion until the referee has called the score or "second serve". The serve is started from any place within the service zone. (Certain drive serves are an exception, see Rule 4.6.) Neither the ball, nor any part of either foot may extend beyond either line of the service zone when initiating the service motion. Stepping on, but not over, the lines is permitted. When completing the service motion, the server may step over the service (front) line provided that some part of both feet remain on or inside the line until the served ball passes the short line. The server may not step over the short line until the ball passes the short line. See Rules 4.10(a) and 4.11(k) for penalties for violations.

Rule 4.3. MANNER

After taking a set position inside the service zone, a player may begin the service motion — any continuous movement which results in the ball being served. Once the service motion begins, the ball must be bounced on the floor in the zone and be struck by the racquet before it bounces a second time. After being struck, the ball must hit the front wall first and on the rebound hit the floor behind the back edge of the short line, either with or without touching one of the side walls.

Rule 4.4. READINESS

Serves shall not begin until the referee has called the score or the second serve and the server has visually checked the receiver. The referee shall call the score as both server and receiver prepare to return to their respective position, shortly after the previous rally has ended.

Rule 4.5. DELAYS

Except as noted in Rule 4.5(b), delays exceeding 10 seconds shall result in an out if the server is the offender or a point if the receiver is the offender.

(a) The 10-second rule is applicable to the server and receiver simultaneously. Collectively, they are allowed up to 10 seconds, after the score is called, to serve or be ready to receive. It is the server's responsibility to look and be certain the receiver is ready. If the receiver is not ready, he must signal so by raising his racquet above his head or completely turning his back to the server. (These are the only two acceptable signals.)

(b) If the server serves the ball while the receiver is signaling *not ready*, the serve shall go over with no penalty and the server shall be warned by the referee to check the receiver. If the server continues to serve without checking the receiver, the referee may award a technical for delay of the game.

(c) After the score is called, if the server looks at the receiver and the receiver is not signaling *not ready*, the server may then serve. If the receiver attempts to signal *not ready* after that point, the signal shall not be acknowledged and the serve becomes legal.

Rule 4.6. DRIVE SERVICE ZONES

The drive serve lines will be three feet from each side wall in the service box, dividing the service area into two 17-foot service zones for drive serves only. The player may drive serve to the same side of the court on which he is standing so long as the start and finish of the service motion takes place outside the three-foot line. The call, or non-call, may be appealed.

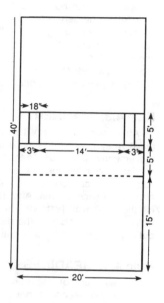

(a) The drive serve zones are not observed for cross-court drive serves, the hard-Z, soft-Z, lob or half-lob serves.

(b) The racquet may not break the plane of the 17-foot zone while making contact with the ball.

(c) The three-foot line is not part of the 17-foot zone. Dropping the ball on the line or standing on the line while serving to the same side is an infraction.

Rule 4.7. SERVE IN DOUBLES

(a) **Order of Serve.** Each team shall inform the referee of the order of service which shall be followed throughout that game. The order of serve may be changed between games. At the beginning of each game, when the first server of the first team to serve is out, the team is out. Thereafter, both players on each team shall serve until the team receives a handout and a sideout.

(b) **Partner's Position.** On each serve, the server's partner shall stand erect with back to the side wall and with both feet on the floor within the service box from the moment the server begins service motion until the served ball passes the short line. Violations are called *foot faults*. However, if the server's partner enters the safety zone before the ball passes the short line the server loses service.

Rule 4.8. DEFECTIVE SERVES

Defective serves are of three types resulting in penalties as follows:

(a) **Dead-Ball Serve.** A dead-ball serve results in no penalty and the server is given another serve (without cancelling a prior fault serve.)

(b) **Fault Serve.** Two fault serves result in a handout.

(c) **Out Serve.** An out serve results in a handout.

Rule 4.9. DEAD-BALL SERVES

Dead-ball serves do not cancel any previous fault serve. The following are dead-ball serves:

(a) **Ball Hits Partner.** A serve which strikes the server's partner while in the doubles box is a dead-ball serve. A serve which touches the floor before touching the server's partner is a short serve.

(b) **Court Hinders.** A serve that takes an irregular bounce because it hit a wet spot or an irregular surface on the court is a dead-ball serve. Also, any serve that hits any surface designated by local rules as an obstruction.

(c) **Broken Ball.** If the ball is determined to have broken on the serve, a new ball shall be substituted and the serve shall be replayed, not cancelling any prior fault serve.

Rule 4.10. FAULT SERVES

The following serves are faults and any two in succession result in an out:

(a) **Foot Faults.** A foot fault results when:

  (1) The server does not begin the service motion with both feet in the service zone.

  (2) The server steps completely over the service line (no part of the foot on or inside the service zone) before the served ball crosses the short line.

  (3) In doubles, the server's partner is not in the service box with both feet on the floor and back to the wall from the time the server begins service motion until the ball passes the short line. (See Rule 4.7.(b).)

(b) **Short Service.** A short serve is any served ball that first hits the front wall and, on the rebound, hits the floor on or in front of the short line (with or without touching a side wall).

(c) **Three-Wall Serve.** A three-wall serve is any served ball that first hits the front wall and, on the rebound, strikes both side walls before touching the floor.

(d) **Ceiling Serve.** A ceiling serve is any served ball that first hits the front wall and then touches the ceiling (with or without touching a side wall).

(e) **Long Serve.** A long serve is a served ball that first hits the front wall and rebounds to the back wall before touching the floor (with or without touching a side wall).

(f) **Out-Of-Court Serve.** An out-of-court serve is any served ball that first hits the wall and, before striking the floor, goes out of the court.

(g) **Bouncing Ball Outside Service Zone.** Bouncing the ball outside the service zone as a part of the service motion is a fault serve.

(h) **Illegal Drive Serve.** A drive serve in which the player fails to observe the 17-foot drive service zone outlined in Rule 4.6.

(i) **Screen Serve.** A served ball that first hits the front wall and on the rebound passes so closely to the server, or server's partner in doubles, that it prevents the receiver from having a clear view of the ball. (The receiver is obligated to place himself in good court position, near center court, to obtain that view. The screen serve is the only fault serve which may not be appealed.

Rule 4.11. OUT SERVES

Any of the following serves results in an out:

(a) **Two Consecutive Fault Serves.** See Rule 4.10.

(b) **Failure to Serve.** Failure of server to put the ball into play under Rule 4.5.

(c) **Missed Serve Attempt.** Any attempt to strike the ball that results in a total miss or in the ball touching any part of the server's body. Also, allowing the ball to bounce more than once during the service motion.

(d) **Touched Serve.** Any served ball that on the rebound from the front wall touches the server or server's racquet, or any ball intentionally stopped or caught by the server or server's partner.

(e) **Fake or Balk Serve.** Any movement of the racquet toward the ball during the serve which is non-continuous and done for the purpose of deceiving the receiver. If a balk serve occurs, but the referee believes that no deceit was involved, he has the option of declaring "no serve" and have the serve replayed without penalty.

(f) **Illegal Hit.** An illegal hit includes contacting the ball twice, carrying the ball, or hitting the ball with the handle of the racquet or part of the body or uniform.

(g) **Non-Front Wall Serve.** Any served ball that does not strike the front wall first.

(h) **Crotch Serve.** Any served ball that hits the crotch of the front wall and floor, front wall and side wall, or front wall and ceiling is an out serve (because it did not hit the front wall first). A serve into the crotch of the back wall and floor is a good serve and in play. A served ball that hits the crotch of the side wall and floor behind the short line is in play.

(i) **Out-Of-Order Serve.** In doubles, when either partner serves out-of-order, the points scored by that server will be subtracted and an out serve will be called; if the second server serves out-of-order, the out serve will be applied to the first server and the

second server will resume serving. If the player designated as the first server serves out-of-order, a side-out will be called. In a match with line judges, the referee may enlist their aid to recall the number of points scored out-of-order.

(j) **Ball Hits Partner.** A served ball that hits the doubles partner while outside the doubles box results in loss of serve.

(k) **Safety Zone Violation.** If the server, or doubles partner, enters into the safety zone before the served ball passes the short line, it shall result in the loss of serve.

Rule 4.12. RETURN OF SERVE

(a) **Receiving Position.**

(1) The receiver may not enter the safety zone until the ball bounces or crosses the receiving line.

(2) On the fly return attempt, the receiver may not strike the ball until the ball breaks the plane of the receiving line. The receiver's follow-through may carry the receiver or his racquet past the receiving line.

(3) Neither the receiver nor his racquet may break the plane of the short line, except if the ball is struck after rebounding off the back wall.

(4) Any violation by the receiver results in a point for the server.

(b) **Defective Serve.** A player on the receiving side may not intentionally catch or touch a served ball (such as an apparently long or short serve) until the referee has made a call or the ball has touched the floor for a second time. Violation results in a point.

(c) **Legal Return.** After a legal serve, a player on the receiving team must strike the ball on the fly or after the first bounce, and before the ball touches the floor the second time; and return the ball to the front wall, either directly or after touching one or both side walls, the back wall or the ceiling, or any combination of those surfaces. A returned ball must touch the front wall before touching the floor.

(d) **Failure to Return.** The failure to return a serve results in a point for the server.

Rule 4.13. CHANGES OF SERVE

(a) **Outs.** A server is entitled to continue serving until:

(1) **Out Serve.** See Rule 4.11.

(2) **Two Consecutive Fault Serves.** See Rule 4.10.

(3) **Ball Hits Partner.** Player hits partner with attempted return.

(4) **Failure to Return Ball.** Player, or partner, fails to keep the ball in play as required by Rule 4.12.(c).

(5) **Avoidable Hinder.** Player or partner commits an avoidable hinder which results in an out. See Rule 4.16.

(b) **Sideout.** In singles, retiring the server is a sideout. In doubles the side is retired when both partners have lost service, except: the team which serves first at the beginning of each game loses serve when the first server is retired. (See Rule 4.7.)

(c) **Effect of Sideout.** When the server (or the serving team) receives a sideout, the server becomes the receiver and the receiver becomes the server.

Rule 4.14. RALLIES

All of the play which occurs after the successful return of serve is called the rally. Play shall be conducted according to the following rules:

(a) **Legal Hits.** Only the head of the racquet may be used at any time to return the ball. The racquet may be held in one or both hands. Switching hands to hit a ball, touching the ball with any part of the body or uniform, or removing the wrist thong results in a loss of the rally.

(b) **One Touch.** The player or team trying to return the ball may touch or strike the ball only once or else the rally is lost. The ball may not be *carried.* (A carried ball is one which rests on the racquet in such a way that the effect is more of a sling or throw than a hit.)

(c) **Failure to Return.** Any of the following constitutes a failure to make a legal return during a rally:

(1) The ball bounces on the floor more than once before being hit.

(2) The ball does not reach the front wall on the fly.

(3) The ball caroms off a player's racquet into a gallery or wall opening without first hitting the front wall.

(4) A ball which obviously did not have the velocity or direction to hit the front wall strikes another player on the court.

(5) A ball struck by one player on a team, hits that player or that player's partner.

(6) Committing a point hinder (Rule 4.16.).

(7) Switching hands during a rally.

(8) Failure to use wrist thong on racquet.

(9) Touching the ball with the body or uniform.

(10) Carry or sling the ball with the racquet.

(d) **Effect of Failure to Return.** Violations of rules (a), (b) or (c) above result in a loss of rally. If the serving player or team loses the rally, it is an *out* (handout or sideout). If the receiver loses the rally, it results in a point for the server.

(e) **Return Attempts.**

(1) In singles, if a player swings at the ball and misses it, the player may continue to attempt to return the ball until it touches the floor for the second time.

(2) In doubles, if one player swings at the ball and misses it, both partners may make further attempts to return the ball until it touches the floor the second time. Both partners on a side are entitled to return the ball.

(f) **Out-Of-Court Ball.**

(1) **After Return.** Any ball returned to the front wall which, on the rebound or the first bounce, goes into the gallery or through any opening in a side-wall shall be declared dead and the server shall receive two serves.

(2) **No Return.** Any ball not returned to the front wall, but which caroms off a player's racquet into the gallery or into any opening in a sidewall either with or without touching the ceiling, side wall, or back wall, shall be an out for the player failing to make the return, or a point for the opponent.

(g) **Broken Ball.** If there is any suspicion that a ball has broken during a rally, play shall continue until the end of the rally. The referee or any player may request the ball be examined. If the referee decides the ball is broken the ball will be replaced and the rally replayed. The server will get two serves. The only proper way to check for a broken ball is to squeeze it by hand. (Checking the ball by striking it with a racquet will not be considered a valid check and shall work to the disadvantage of the player or team which struck the ball after the rally.)

(h) **Play Stoppage.**

(1) If a foreign object enters the court, or any other outside interference occurs, the referee shall stop the play.

(2) If a player loses a shoe or other properly worn equipment, the referee shall stop the play if the occurrence interferes with ensuing play or player's safety; however, safety permitting, the offensive player is entitled to one opportunity to hit a rally ending shot. (See Rule 14.16.(i.).)

(i) **Replays.** Whenever a rally is replayed for any reason, the server is awarded two serves. A previous fault serve is not considered.

Rule 4.15. DEAD-BALL HINDERS

A rally is replayed without penalty and the server receives two serves whenever a dead-ball hinder occurs.

(a) **Situations.**

(1) **Court Hinders.** The referee should stop play immediately whenever the ball hits any part of

the court that was designated in advance as a court hinder (such as a door handle). The referee should also stop play (i) when the ball takes an irregular bounce as a result of contacting a rough surface (such as court light or vent) or after striking a wet spot on the floor or wall and (ii) when, in the referee's opinion, the irregular bounce affected the rally. A court hinder is the only type of hinder that is appealable. See rule 3.7.(a).

(2) **Ball Hits Opponent.** When an opponent is hit by a return shot in flight, it is a dead-ball hinder. If the opponent is struck by a ball which obviously did not have the velocity or direction to reach the front wall, it is not a hinder, and the player that hit the ball will lose the rally. A player who has been hit by the ball can stop play and make the call, though the call must be made immediately and acknowledged by the referee.

(3) **Body Contact.** If body contact occurs which the referee believes was sufficient to stop the rally, either for the purpose of preventing injury by further contact or because the contact prevented a player from being able to make a reasonable return, the referee shall call a hinder. Incidental body contact in which the offensive player clearly will have the advantage should not be called a hinder, unless the offensive player obviously stops play. Contact with the racquet on the follow-through normally is not considered a dead-ball hinder.

(4) **Screen Ball.** Any ball rebounding from the front wall so close to the body of the defensive team that it interferes with, or prevents, the offensive player from having clear view of the ball. (The referee should be careful not to make the screen call so quickly that it takes away a good offensive opportunity.) A ball that passes between the legs of the side that just returned the ball is not automatically a screen. It depends on the proximity of the players. Again, the call should work to the advantage of the offensive player.

(5) **Backswing Hinder.** Any body or racquet contact, on the backswing or en route to or just prior to returning the ball, which impairs the hitter's ability to take a reasonable swing. This call can be made by the player attempting the return, though the call must be made immediately and is subject to the referee's approval. Note the interference may be considered an avoidable hinder. (See Rule 4.16.)

(6) **Safety Holdup.** Any player about to execute a return who believes he is likely to strike his opponent with the ball or racquet may immediately stop play and request a dead-ball hinder. This call must be made immediately and is subject to

acceptance and approval of the referee. (The referee will grant a dead-ball hinder if he believes the holdup was reasonable and the player would have been able to return the shot, and the referee may also call an avoidable hinder if warranted.)

(7) **Other Interference.** Any other unintentional interference which prevents an opponent from having a fair chance to see or return the ball. Example: When a ball from another court enters the court during a rally or when a referee's call on an adjacent court obviously distracts a player.

(b) **Effect of Hinders.** The referee's call of hinder stops play and voids any situation which follows, such as the ball hitting the player. The only hinders that may be called by a player are described in rules (2), (5), and (6) above, and all of these are subject to the approval of the referee. A dead-ball hinder stops play and the rally is replayed. The server receives two serves.

(c) **Avoidance.** While making an attempt to return the ball, a player is entitled to a fair chance to see and return the ball. It is the responsibility of the side that has just hit the ball to move so the receiving side may go straight to the ball and have an unobstructed view of the ball. In the judgment of the referee however, the receiver must make a reasonable effort to move towards the ball and have a reasonable chance to return the ball in order for a hinder to be called.

Rule 4.16. AVOIDABLE HINDERS

An avoidable hinder results in the loss of the rally. An avoidable hinder does not necessarily have to be an intentional act and is the result of any of the following:

(a) **Failure to Move.** A player does not move sufficiently to allow an opponent a shot straight to the front wall as well as a cross-court shot which is a shot directly to the front wall at an angle that would cause the ball to rebound directly to the rear corner farthest from the player hitting the ball. Also when a player moves in such a direction that it prevents an opponent from taking either of these shots.

(b) **Stroke Interference.** This occurs when a player moves, or fails to move, so that the opponent returning the ball does not have a free, unimpeded swing. This includes unintentionally moving the wrong direction which prevents an opponent from making an open offensive shot.

(c) **Blocking.** Moves into a position which blocks the opponent from getting to, or returning, the ball; or in doubles, a player moves in front of an opponent as the player's partner is returning the ball.

(d) **Moving into the Ball.** Moves in the way and is struck by the ball just played by the opponent.

(e) **Pushing.** Deliberately pushes or shoves opponent during a rally.

(f) **Intentional Distractions.** Deliberate shouting, stamping of feet, waving of racquet, or any other manner of disrupting one's opponent.

(g) **View Obstruction.** A player moves across an opponent's line of vision just before the opponent strikes the ball.

(h) **Wetting the Ball.** The players, particularly the server, should insure that the ball is dry prior to the serve. Any wet ball that is not corrected prior to the serve shall result in an avoidable hinder against the server.

(i) **Equipment.** The loss of any improperly worn equipment, or equipment not required on court, which interferes with the play of the ball or safety of the players is an avoidable hinder. Examples of this include the loss of improperly fastened eyewear and hand towels. (See Rule 4.14.(h).)

Rule 4.17. TIMEOUTS

(a) **Rest Periods.** Each player or team is entitled to three 30-second timeouts in games to 15 and two 30-second timeouts in games to 11. Timeouts may not be called by either side after service motion has begun. Calling for a timeout when none remain or after service motion has begun, or taking more than 30 seconds in a timeout, will result in the assessment of a technical for delay of game.

(b) **Injury.** If a player is injured during the course of a match as a result of contact, such as with the ball, racquet, wall, or floor, he will be awarded an injury timeout. While a player may call more than one timeout for the same injury or for additional injuries which occur during the match, a player is not allowed more than a total of 15 minutes of rest during a match. If the injured player is not able to resume play after total rest of 15 minutes, the match shall be awarded to the opponent. Muscle cramps and pulls, fatigue, and other ailments that are not caused by direct contact on the court will not be considered an injury.

(c) **Equipment Timeouts.** Players are expected to keep all clothing and equipment in good, playable condition and are expected to use regular timeouts and time between games for adjustment and replacement of equipment. If a player or team is out of timeouts and the referee determines that an equipment change or adjustment is necessary for fair and safe continuation of the match, the referee may award an equipment timeout not to exceed two minutes. The referee may allow additional time under unusual circumstances.

(d) **Between Games.** The rest period between the first two games of a match is two minutes. If a tiebreaker is necessary, the rest period between the second and third game is five minutes.

(e) **Postponed Games.** Any games postponed by referees shall be resumed with the same score as when postponed.

Rule 4.18. TECHNICALS

(a) **Technical Fouls.** The referee is empowered to deduct one point from a player's or team's score when, in the referee's sole judgment, the player is being overtly and deliberately abusive. The actual invoking of this penalty is called a Referee's Technical. If the player or team against whom the technical was assessed does not resume play immediately, the referee is empowered to forfeit the match in favor of the opponent. Some examples of actions which may result in technicals are:

(1) Excessive arguing.

(2) Threat of any nature to opponent or referee.

(3) Excessive or hard striking of the ball between rallies.

(4) Slamming of the racquet against walls or floor, slamming the door, or any action which might result in injury to the court or other players.

(5) Delay of game. Examples include (i) serving before the receiver is ready, (ii) taking too much time to dry the court, (iii) questioning of the referee excessively about the rules, (iv) exceeding the time allotted for timeouts or between games, or (v) calling a timeout when none remain.

(6) Intentional front line foot faults to negate a bad lob serve.

(7) Anything considered to be unsportsmanlike behavior.

(8) Failure to wear lensed eyewear designed for racquet sports is an automatic technical on the first infraction and a mandatory timeout will be charged against the offending player to acquire the proper eyewear. A second infraction by that player during the match will result in automatic forfeiture of the match.

(b) **Technical Warning.** If a player's behavior is not so severe as to warrant a referee's technical, a technical warning may be issued without point deduction.

(c) **Effect of Technical or Warning.** If a referee issues a referee's technical, one point shall be removed from the offender's score. If a referee issues a technical warning, it shall not result in a loss of rally or point and shall be accompanied by a brief explanation of the reason for the warning. The awarding of the technical shall have no effect on service changes or sideouts. If the technical occurs either between games or when the offender has no points, the result will be that the offender's score will revert to a minus (-1).

Rule 4.19. PROFESSIONAL

A professional is defined as any player who has accepted prize money regardless of the amount in any PRO SANCTIONED (including WPRA and RMA) tournament or in any other tournament so deemed by the AARA board of directors. (Note: Any player concerned about the adverse effect of losing amateur status should contact the AARA National Office at the earliest opportunity to ensure a clear understanding of this rule and that no action is taken that could jeopardize that status.)

(a) An amateur player may participate in a PRO SANCTIONED tournament but will not be considered a professional (i) if no prize money is accepted or (ii) if the prize money received remains intact and placed in trust under AARA guidelines.

(b) The acceptance of merchandise or travel expenses shall not be considered prize money, and thus does not jeopardize a player's amateur status.

Rule 4.20. RETURN TO AMATEUR STATUS

Any player who has been classified as a professional can recover amateur status by requesting, in writing, this desire to be reclassified as an amateur. This application shall be tendered to the Executive Director of the AARA or his designated representative, and shall become effective immediately as long as the player making application for reinstatement of amateur status has received no money in any tournament, as defined in Rule 4.19. for the past 12 months.

Rule 4.21. AGE GROUP DIVISIONS

Age is determined as of the first day of the tournament:

(a) **Men's and Women's Age Divisions:**
    Open — All players other than Pro
    Junior Veterans — 19+
    Junior Veterans — 25+
    Veterans — 30+
    Seniors — 35+
    Veteran Seniors — 40+
    Masters — 45+
    Veteran Masters — 50+
    Golden Masters — 55+
    Senior Golden Masters — 60+
    Veteran Golden Masters — 65+
    Advanced Golden Masters — 70+
    Super Golden Masters — 75+
    Grand Masters — 80+

(b) **Other Divisions.**
    Doubles
    Mixed Doubles
    Wheelchair
    Visually Impaired

(c) **Junior Divisions.** Age determined as of January 1st of each calendar year. Junior Boy's and Girl's age divisions:
    18 & Under
    16 & Under
    14 & Under
    12 & Under
    10 & Under
    8 & Under
    8 & Under Multi-Bounce
    Doubles
    Mixed Doubles

Rule 4.22. EIGHT AND UNDER MULTI-BOUNCE MODIFICATIONS

In general, the AARA's standard rules governing racquetball play will be followed except for the modifications which follow.

(a) **Basic Return Rule.** In general, the ball remains in play as long as it is bouncing. However, the player may swing only once at the ball and the ball is considered dead at the point it stops bouncing and begins to roll. Also, anytime the ball rebounds off the back wall, it must be struck before it crosses the short line enroute to the front wall, except as explained in the Blast Rule.

(b) **Blast Rule.** if the ball caroms from the front wall to the back wall on the fly, the player may hit the ball from any place on the court — including past the short line — so long as the ball is bouncing.

(c) **Front Wall Lines.** Two parallel lines (tape may be used) should be placed across the front wall such that the bottom edge of one line is three feet above the floor and the bottom edge of the other line is one foot above the floor. During the rally, any ball that hits the front wall (i) below the three foot line and (ii) either on or above the one-foot line must be returned before it bounces a third time. However, if the ball hits below the one-foot line, it must be returned before it bounces twice. If the ball hits on or above the three-foot line, the ball must be returned as described in the basic return rule.

(d) **Games and Matches.** All games are played to 11 points and the first side to win two games, wins the match.

5 — TOURNAMENTS

Rule 5.1. DRAWS

(a) If possible, all draws shall be made at least two days before the tournament commences. The seeding method of drawing shall be approved by the AARA.

(b) The draw and seeding committee shall be chaired by teh AARA's Executive Director, National Commissioner and the host tournament director. No other persons shall participate in the draw or seeding unless at the invitation of the draw and seeding committee.

(c) In local and regional tournaments the draw shall be the responsibility of the tournament director. In regional play, the tournament director should work in coordination with the AARA Regional Commissioner at the tournament.

Rule 5.2. SCHEDULING

(a) **Preliminary Matches.** If one or more contestants are entered in both singles and doubles, they may be required to play both singles and doubles on the same day or night with little rest between matches. This is a risk assumed on entering two singles events or a singles and doubles event. If possible, the schedule should provide at least one hour rest period between matches.

(b) **Final Matches.** Where one or more players has reached the finals in both singles and doubles, it is recommended that the doubles match be played on the day preceding the singles. This would assure more rest between the final matches. If both final matches must be played on the same day or night, the following procedure is recommended:

(1) The singles match be played first.

(2) A rest period of not less than one hour be allowed between the finals in singles and doubles.

Rule 5.3. NOTICE OF MATCHES

After the first round of matches, it is the reponsibility of each player to check the posted schedules to determine the time and place of each subsequent match. If any change is made in the schedule after posting, it shall be the duty of the committee or tournament director to notify the players of the change.

Rule 5.4. THIRD PLACE

Players are not required to play off for 3rd place or 4th place. However, for point standings, if one semifinalist wants to play off for third and the other semifinalist does not, the one willing to play shall be awarded third place. If both semifinalists do not wish to play off for 3rd or 4th position, then the points shall be awarded evenly.

Rule 5.5. ROUND ROBIN SCORING

The position of players or teams in round robin competition is determined by the following sequence:

(a) Winner of the most matches;

(b) In a two-way tie, winner of the head-to-head match prevails;

(c) In a tie of three or more, the player who lost the fewest games is awarded the highest position;

(1) If a two-way tie results, revert to No. (b);

(2) If a multiple tie remains, total points scored against the player in all matches will be tabulated. The player with the least points scored against will prevail.

NOTE: Forfeits will count as a match won in two games. In cases where points score against is the tiebreaker, the points scored by the forfeiting team will be discounted from consideration of points scored against all teams.

Rule 5.6. AARA REGIONAL TOURNAMENTS

The United States and Europe are divided into 16 regions as specified in rule 5.11.(c).

(a) A player may compete in only one regional singles and one regional doubles tournament per year.

(b) The defined area of eligibility for a person's region is that of their permanent residence. Players are encouraged to participate in their own region; however, for the purpose of convenience players may participate outside their region.

(c) A player can participate in only two championship events in a regional tournament.

(d) Awards and remuneration to the AARA National Championships will be posted on the entry blank.

Rule 5.7. TOURNAMENT MANAGEMENT

In all AARA sanctioned tournaments, the tournament director and/or the national AARA official in attendance may decide on a change of court after the completion of any tournament game, if such a change will accommodate better spectator conditions.

Rule 5.8. TOURNAMENT CONDUCT

In all AARA sanctioned tournaments, the referee is empowered to default a match, if the conduct of a player or team is considered detrimental to the tournament and the game. (See Rule 3.5.(d) and 3.5.(e).)

Rule 5.9. AARA ELIGIBILITY

(a) Any current AARA member who has not been classified as a professional (see Rule 4.19) may compete in any AARA sanctioned tournament.

(b) Any current AARA member who has been classified as a professional may compete in any AARA sanctioned event that offers prize money or merchandise.

RULE 5.10. DIVISION COMPETITION

Men and women may compete only in events for their respective sex during Regional and National Championships. If there is not sufficient number of players to warrant play in a specific division, the tournament director may place the entrants in a comparably competitive division. Note: For the purpose of encouraging the development of women's racquetball, the governing bodies of numerous states permit women to play in men's division when a comparable skill level isn't available in the women's division.

Rule 5.11. U.S. NATIONAL CHAMPIONSHIPS

The National Singles, Junior and National Doubles are separate tournaments and are played on different weekends. There will be a consolation round in all divisions.

(a) **Regional Qualifications.**

    (1) The National Ratings Committee may handle the rating of each region and determine how many players shall qualify from each regional tournament.

    (2) AARA National Champions are exempt from qualifying for the following year's National Championship.

    (3) There may be a tournament one day ahead of the National Tournament at the same site to qualify 8 players in each division who were unable to qualify or who failed to qualify in the Regionals. This rule is in force only when a region is obviously over subscribed.

(b) **Definition of Regions.**

    (1) Qualifying Singles. A player may have to qualify at one of the 17 regional tournaments.

    (2) Qualifying Doubles. There will be no regional qualifying for doubles.

(c) **AARA Regions.**

    (1) Maine, New Hampshire, Vermont, Massachusetts, Rhode Island, Connecticut

    (2) New York, New Jersey

    (3) Pennsylvania, Maryland, Virginia, Delaware, District of Columbia

    (4) Florida, Georgia

    (5) Alabama, Mississippi, Tennessee

    (6) Arkansas, Kansas, Missouri, Oklahoma

    (7) Texas, Louisiana

    (8) Wisconsin, Iowa, Illinois

    (9) West Virginia, Ohio, Michigan

    (10) Indiana, Kentucky

    (11) North Dakota, South Dakota, Minnesota, Nebraska

    (12) Arizona, New Mexico, Utah, Colorado

    (13) Montana, Wyoming

    (14) California, Hawaii, Nevada

    (15) Washington, Idaho, Oregon, Alaska

    (16) Americans in Europe

    (17) North Carolina, South Carolina

Rule 5.12. U.S. NATIONAL JUNIOR OLYMPIC CHAMPIONSHIP

It will be conducted on a separate date and at a separate location under the same parameters provided in Rules 5.11(a) and 5.11(b).

Rule 5.13. U.S. NATIONAL INTERCOLLEGIATE CHAMPIONSHIPS

It will be conducted on a separate date and at a separate location.

6 — NATIONAL WHEELCHAIR RACQUETBALL ASSOCIATION MODIFICATIONS

Rule 6.1. CHANGES TO STANDARD RULES

In general, the AARA's standard rules governing racquetball play will be followed except for the modifications which follow.

(a) Where the AARA Rulebook rules refer to server, person, body or other similar variations, for wheelchair play such reference shall include all parts of the wheelchair in addition to the person sitting on it.

(b) Where the rules refer to feet, standing or other similar descriptions, for wheelchair play it means only where the rear wheels actually touch the floor.

(c) Where the rules mention body contact, for wheelchair play it shall mean any part of the wheelchair in addition to the player.

(d) Where the rules refer to *double bounce* or after the first bounce, it shall mean three bounces. All variations of the same phrases shall be revised accordingly.

Rule 6.2. DIVISIONS

(a) **Novice Division.** The novice division is for the beginning player who is just learning to play.

(b) **Intermediate Division.** The Intermediate Division is for the player who has played tournaments before and has a skill level to be competitive in the division.

(c) **Open Division.** The Open Division is the highest level of play and is for the advanced player.

(d) **Multi-Bounce Division.** The Multi-Bounce Division is for the individuals (men or women) whose mobility is such that wheelchair racquetball would be impossible if not for the Multi-Bounce Division.

(e) **Junior Division.** The junior divisions are for players who are under the age of 19. The tournament director will determine if the divisions will be played as two-bounce or multi-bounce. Age divisions re: 8-11, 12-15, and 16-18.

Rule 6.3. RULES

(a) **Two-Bounce Rule.** Two bounces are used in wheelchair racquetball in all divisions except the Multi-Bounce Division. The ball may hit the floor twice before being returned.

(b) **Out of Chair Rule.** The player can neither intentionally jump out of his chair to hit a ball nor stand up in his chair to serve the ball. If the referee determines that the chair was left intentionally it will result in loss of the rally for the offender. If a player unintentionally leaves his chair, no penalty will be assessed. Repeat offenders will be warned by the referee.

(c) **Equipment Standards.** In order to protect playing surfaces, the tournament officials may not allow a person to participate with black tires or anything which will mark or damage the court.

(d) **Start.** The serve may be started from any place within the service zone. Although the front casters may extend beyond the lines of the service zone, at no time shall the rear wheels cross either the service or short line before the served ball crosses the short line. Penalties for violation are the same as those for the standard game.

(e) **Maintenance Delay.** A maintenance delay is a delay in the progress of a match due to a malfunction of a wheelchair, prosthesis, or assistive device. Such delay must be requested by the player, granted by the referee during the match, and shall not exceed five minutes. Only two such delays may be granted for each player for each match. After using both maintenance delays the player has the following options:

(1) Continue play with the defective equipment.
(2) Immediately substitute replacement equipment.
(3) Postponement of game, with the approval of the referee and opponent.

Rule 6.4. MULTI-BOUNCE RULES

(a) The ball may bounce as many times as the receiver wants though the player may swing only once to return the ball to the front wall.

(b) The ball must be hit before it crosses the short line on its way back to the front wall.

(c) The receiver cannot cross the short line after the ball contacts the back wall.

7 — VISUALLY IMPAIRED MODIFICATIONS

In general, the AARA's standard rules governing racquetball play will be followed except for the modifications which follow.

Rule 7.1. ELIGIBILITY

A player's visual acuity must not be better than 20/200 with the best practical eye correction or else the player's field of vision must not be better than 20 degrees. The three classifications of blindness are B-1 (totally blind to light perception), B-2 (able to see hand movement up to 20/600 corrected), and B-3 (from 20/600 to 20/200 corrected).

Rule 7.2. RETURN OF SERVE AND RALLIES

On the return of serve and on every return thereafter, the player may make multiple attempts to strike the ball until (i) the ball has been touched, (ii) the ball has stopped bouncing, or (iii) the ball has passed the short line after touching the back wall. The only exception is described in Rule 7.3.

Rule 7.3. BLAST RULE

If the ball (other than on the serve) caroms from the front wall to the back wall on the fly, the player may retrieve the ball from any place on the court — including in front of the short line — so long as the ball has not been touched and is still bouncing.

Rule 7.4. HINDERS

A hinder will result in the rally being replayed without penalty unless the hinder was intentional. If a hinder is clearly an intentional hinder, an avoidable hinder should be called and the rally awarded to the non-offending player or team.

8 — WOMEN'S PROFESSIONAL RACQUETBALL ASSOCIATION MODIFICATION

In general, the AARA's standard rules governing racquetball play will be followed except for the modifications which follow.

Rule 8.1. MATCH, GAME, SUPER TIEBREAKER

A match is won by the first side winning three games. All games, other than the fifth one, are won by the first side to score 11 points. The fifth game, which is called the Super Tiebreaker, is won by the first side scoring 11 points and having at least a two-point lead. If necessary, the game will continue beyond 11 points until such time as one side has a two-point lead.

Rule 8.2. APPEALS

There is NO limit on the number of appeals that a player or team may make.

Rule 8.3. SERVE

The server may leave the service zone as soon as the serve has been made.

Rule 8.4. DRIVE SERVICE ZONE

The server may begin a drive serve anywhere in the service zone so long as the server is completely inside the 17-foot drive service zone when the ball is actually contacted.

Rule 8.5. RETURN OF SERVE

The receiver may enter the safety zone as soon as the ball has been served. The served ball may not be contacted in the receiving zone until it has bounced. Neither the receiver nor the receiver's racquet may break the plane of the short line unless the ball is struck after rebounding off the back wall. On the fly return attempt, the receiver may not strike the ball until the ball breaks the plane of the receiving line. The receiver's follow-through may carry the receiver or the racquet past the receiving line.

Rule 8.6. AVOIDABLE HINDER

An avoidable hinder should be called only if the player's movement or failure to move interfered with the opponent's opportunity to take an offensive shot.

Rule 8.7. TIMEOUTS

Each player or team is entitled to two 30-second time-outs per game.

Rule 8.8. TIME BETWEEN GAMES

The rest period between all games will be 2 minutes except that a 5-minute rest period will be allowed between the fourth and fifth games.

9 — ONE-WALL AND THREE-WALL MODIFICATIONS

In general, the AARA's standard rules governing racquetball play will be followed except for the modifications which follow.

(a) **One Wall.** There are two playing surfaces, the front wall and the floor. The wall is 20 feet wide and 16 feet high. The floor is 20 feet wide and 34 feet to the back edge of the long line. To permit movement by players, there should be a minimum of three feet (six feet is recommended) beyond the long line and six feet outside each side line.

    (1) **Short line.** The back edge of the short line is 16 feet from the wall.

    (2) **Service Markers.** Lines at least six inches long which are parallel with, and midway between, the long and short lines. The extension of the service markers form the imaginary boundary of the service line.

    (3) **Service Zone.** The entire floor area inside and including the short line, side lines and service line.

    (4) **Receiving Zone.** The entire floor area in back of the short line, including the side lines and the long line.

(b) **Three-Wall with Short Side Wall.** The front wall is 20 feet wide and 20 feet high. The side walls are 20 feet long and 20 feet high, though the sidewall tapers down to 12 feet high. The floor length and court markings are the same as for four-wall.

(c) **Three-Wall with Long-Side Wall.** The court is 20 feet wide, 20 feet high and 40 feet long. The side walls may taper from 20 feet high at the front wall down to 12 feet high at the end of the court. All court markings are the same as four-wall.

(d) **Service in Three-Wall Courts.** A serve that goes beyond the side walls on the fly is considered long. A serve that goes beyond the long line on a fly, but within the side walls, is the same as a short.

10 — HOW TO REFEREE WHEN THERE IS NO REFEREE

SAFETY IS THE RESPONSIBILITY OF EVERY PLAYER WHO ENTERS THE COURT

At no time should the physical safety of the participants be compromised. Players are entitled, and expected, to hold up their swing, *without penalty*, any time they believe there might be a risk of physical contact. Any time a player says he held up to avoid contact, even if he was over-cautious, he is entitled to a hinder (rally replayed without penalty).

SCORE

Since there is no referee, or scorekeeper, it is important for the server to announce both the server's and receiver's score before *every* first serve.

DURING RALLIES

During rallies, it is the *hitter's* responsibility to make the call. If there is a possibility of a skip ball, double-bounce, or illegal hit, play should continue until the hitter makes the call against himself. If the hitter does not make the call against himself and goes on to win the rally, and the player thought that one of the hitter's shots was not good, he may *appeal* to the hitter by pointing out which shot he thought was bad and request the hitter to reconsider. If the hitter is sure of his call, and the opponent is still sure the hitter is wrong, the rally is replayed. As a matter of etiquette, players are expected to make calls against themselves any time they are not sure. Unless the hitter is certain the shot was good, he should call it a skip.

SERVICE

(a) **Fault Serves.** The receiver has the primary responsibility to make these calls, though either player may make the call. The receiver must make the call immediately, and not wait until he hits the ball and has the benefit of seeing how good a shot he can hit. *It is not an option play.* The receiver does not have the right to play a short serve just because he thinks it's a setup.

(b) **Screen Serves.** When there is no referee, the screen serve call is the sole responsibility of the receiver. If the receiver has taken the proper court position, near center court, does not have clear view of the ball the screen should be called *immediately.* The receiver may not call a screen after attempting to hit the ball or, after taking himself out of proper court position by starting the wrong way. *The server may not call a screen under any circumstances* and must expect to play the rally unless he hears a call from the receiver.

(c) **Other Situations.** Foot faults, 10-second violations, receiving line violations, service zone infringement, and other technical calls really require a referee. However, if either player believes his opponent is abusing any of the rules, be sure there is agreement on what the rule is, and to put each other on notice that the rules should be followed.

HINDERS

Generally, the hinder should work like the screen serve — as an option play for the hindered party. *Only the person going for the shot can stop play by calling a hinder, and he must do so immediately* — not wait until he has the benefit of seeing how good a shot he can hit. If the hindered party believes he can make an effective return in spite of some physical contact or screen that has occurred, he may continue to play.

AVOIDABLE HINDERS

Since avoidable hinders are usually unintentional, they can occur even in the friendliest matches. A player who realizes that he caused such a hinder should simply declare his opponent to be the winner of the rally. If a player feels that his opponent caused such a hinder, but the opponent does not make the call on himself, the offended player should point out that he thought that an avoidable hinder occurred.

However, unless the opponent agrees that a point hinder occurred, none will be called. Often just pointing out what appears to have been a point hinder will prevent the opponent from such actions on future rallies.

DISPUTES

If either player, for any reason desires to have a referee, it is considered common courtesy for the other player to go along with the request, and a referee suitable to both sides should be found. If there is not a referee, and a question about a rule or rule interpretation comes up, seek out the club pro or a more experienced player. Then, after the match, contact your state racquetball association for the answer.

Index

A

around-the-wall ball, 49

B

backhand stroke, 21
  backswing, 22
  contact with the ball, 24
  follow-through, 24
  forward swing, 23
  wrist cock, 22
back wall, 65, 70
  advantage, 66
Battleball, 65
blocking, 86, 107

C

ceiling shot,
  ceiling-front wall, 44
  front wall-ceiling, 41
concentration, 10, 75
continental grip, 13
corner shots, 72
court dimensions and markings, 1-2
court etiquette, 103
  application of warm-up, 103
  common faults, 105
  hinders, 107
  sportsmanship, 114
cross-stepping, 17
crotch shots, 111
cutthroat, 1, 112, 113

D

defensive game, 81
defensive shots, 41
  ceiling shot, 41, 44
  ceiling-front wall, 44
  drills, 96
  front wall-ceiling, 41
  high Z, 47
  lob, 45
doubles, 1, 112
drills, 91-102
  backhand shots, 93, 94
  back wall, 97
  ceiling shots, 99
  corner return, 98
  defensive return game, 102
  defensive shots, 96
  forehand shots, 93, 94
  game warm-up, 102
  high-Z, 95
  lob, 95
  mini game, 101
  offensive shots, 99, 100
  rally, 101
  serving, 96
  suicide, 94
  thirty-second, 95
  watching the game, 92
drive serve, 55
drive serve zone, 55

E

eastern,
  backhand, 12
  forehand, 11
equipment, 3
etiquette, 103, 105, 110

F

fault, 105
  long, 105
  short, 105
  two walls, 105
foot movement,
  cross-stepping, 17
  pivot, 16
forehand stroke, 18
  backswing, 18
  contact with the ball, 19
  follow-through, 21
  forward swing, 19
  wrist cock, 18
"frying pan" grip, 14

G

garbage serve, 61
glossary of terms, 115
grips,
  continental, 13
  eastern backhand, 12
  eastern forehand, 11
  trigger, 11
  western, 14

H

high Z serve, 57
high Z shot, 47
hinders, 107-111
  avoidable, 107
  dead ball, 107,109
hitting into the back wall, 70

I

interpreting the rules, 103
  ball in play, 106
  cutthroat, 113
  doubles, 112
  fault, 105
  hinders, 107

keeping score, 105
miscellaneous rules, 111
serving, 105
use of racquet, 111

K

kill shot, 27
  backhand, 29
  corner kill, 31
  drills, 100
  forehand, 29
  overhead kill, 33
  pinch kill, 31
  straight-in kill, 30

L

legal serve, 1, 52
lob serve, 54
lob shot, 45
low Z serve, 57

M

mental preparation, 10
moving to the ball, 80

N

non-thinking strategy, 75-82
  center court, 77, 79
  concentration, 75
  keeping the ball in play, 91
  leaving the center court to play the ball, 81
  moving to a court position, 79, 81
  moving to the ball, 80
  opponent's errors, 75
  playing a defensive game, 81
  serve, 76

O

object of game, 1
offensive shots, 27
  drills, 99, 100
  kill shots, 27
  passing shots, 35
out serve, 106
outfitting for play, 2
  balls, 4
  clothing, 2
  eyewear, 4

gloves, 3
grip size, 5
headbands, 3
racquets, 4
shoes, 3
strings and tension of strings, 5
wristbands, 3
overhead serve, 59

P

passing shots, 35
cross-court, 37
down-the-line, 36
pass, 35
patience, 65
pivot, 16
preliminaries to racquetball strokes, 9
putting the strokes together,
non-thinking strategy, 75
thinking strategy, 83

R

racquet,
balls, 4
care, 6
grip size, 5
handle and thong, 6
rules, 111
strings and string tension, 5
types, 4
receiving line, 1, 112
relaxation, 9
rules, miscellaneous, 111

S

safety,
protective eyewear, 4, 5
hinder, 7
movement of players on court, 6
opponent's path and position, 6
path of ball, 7
racquet as shield, 7
thong, 6
scoring,
scales, 91
serving and ball in play, 105
service zone, 1, 105

serving, 51
drive, 55
garbage, 61
half lob, 55
high Z, 57
legal serve, 1, 52
lob, 54
low Z, 57
overhead, 59
rules, 105
strategy, 76, 83
Z, 57
set position, 15
"shaking hands", 11
singles, 1
sportsmanship, 114
strategy,
non-thinking, 75
thinking, 83
stretching, 9
strokes,
backhand, 21
defensive, 41
forehand, 18
offensive, 27

T

thinking strategy, 83
anticipation, 85
best offense against a power player, 89
blocking, 86
choosing the right serve, 83
controlling the tempo, 85
good defense as best offense, 89
hitting a winning shot, 88
hit your hardest serve, 84
hustle, 90
keeping the opponent moving, 86
moving the opponent out of the center court, 87
moving to cut off the opponent's return, 87, 88
opponent's backhand, 84
opponent's forehand, 84
playing the weakness, 89
returning to the offense, 87
take away opponent's best shot, 86
using the court wisely, 86
variety in your serve, 83

three-wall shot, 47
trigger trip, 11

U

use of back wall and corners, 65

W

warm-up, 9
   drill, 102
   etiquette, 103
   increase heart rate, 10
   mental preparation, 10
   relaxation, 9
   stretching, 9
   watching the game, 92
western grip, 14
wrist,
   cock, 18
   rotation, 13
   snap, 11